MACCABEE

MACCABEE

AN EPIC IN FREE VERSE

BASED UPON THE BOOKS OF MACCABEES

BY

HOWARD RUBENSTEIN

GRANITE HILLS PRESS™

MACCABEE
AN EPIC IN FREE VERSE
BASED UPON THE BOOKS OF MACCABEES

Published 2004 by

Granite Hills Press™
8677 Villa La Jolla Dr., #1114
La Jolla, CA 92037
granitehillspress@yahoo.com

ISBN: 1-929468-08-3
Library of Congress Control Number: 2004108687

Publisher's Cataloging-in-Publication Data

Rubenstein, Howard S., 1931-
    Maccabee : an epic in free verse based upon the
books of Maccabees / by Howard Rubenstein.
    p. cm.
    Includes bibliographical references.
    LCCN 2004108687
    ISBN 1-929468-08-3

    1. Maccabees--Poetry. 2. Judaism--Poetry.
3. Religious tolerance--Poetry. 4. Theism--Poetry.
I. Title. II. Title: Bible. O.T. Apocrypha. Maccabees.

PS3618.U3167M33 2004   811'.6
                              QBI33-2064

Printed in the United States of America

Dedicated
to the valiant few
who fight the tyranny of the many
for the liberty of all

CONTENTS

CONTENTS

CONTENTS

CONTENTS

ACKNOWLEDGMENTS

It is a pleasure to thank Rebecca Rauff for editing the manuscript; Brian Hiltz for creating the cover; and, as always, my wife, Judy, for her many questions and suggestions, for editing all drafts, and especially for her constant and loving support.

INTRODUCTION

Maccabee is an epic in free verse consisting of twenty-one ballads. It is historical fiction, based mainly on First Maccabees, a historical account of events that took place mostly in Judea during the second century B.C.E. First Maccabees was presumably written in Judea during the second century B.C.E., perhaps by an eyewitness to some of the events. To a lesser extent, *Maccabee* is also based on Second, Third, and Fourth Maccabees, which were presumably written in the second or first century B.C.E.

The four books of Maccabees are in the Apocrypha, a word originally meaning "hidden," because the books were not meant for general consumption. Many people still do not know of the existence of these books or have not read them.

The main purpose of *Maccabee* is to recount the events told in these books in a way that makes them accessible to a general audience, because they are far too important to remain in obscurity. These events describe the first historical fight for religious liberty and set the precedent for everyone who loves liberty. Another purpose of *Maccabee* is to show that Hanukah was created in the context of these events and, therefore, is a holiday of major significance.

LICENSE IN THE NARRATIVE

Maccabee is neither a literal translation of the books of Maccabees nor an exact historical account of the period. Even so, it is faithful to the major events, and I have not taken more license than do other authors of works of historical fiction. Especially germane, because it deals with the same historical period, is Howard Fast's novel *My Glorious Brothers* (Boston: Little, Brown and Company, 1948).

I have developed some historical figures in ways consistent with their historical images, I have invented other figures and also some dialogue and action, I have reconstructed the first celebration of Hanukah based upon information provided in the sources, and I have advanced some religious philosophy consistent with the period and events. Some of this philosophy is probably from the period, even though the sources are not known to me, and some of it may be original with me. I accept responsibility for all of it. I have also added relevant teachings from the Torah and prayers from the Psalms and Prophets. Similarly, I have deleted events I consider extraneous or repetitious.

One historical figure whom I developed requires special comment because he is controversial. Alexander, a son of the tyrant Antiochus Epiphanes (and not to be confused with Alexander the Great, who lived two centuries earlier), is described in the first book of Maccabees as Antiochus Epiphanes' son and legitimate successor as king of Syria. The author of First Maccabees was not alone in this assessment. The Roman Empire also recognized Alexander, as did the king of Egypt. Moreover, First Maccabees portrays Alexander as a man of noble character, who was respectful of the Jews and honorable in his dealings with them.

On the other hand, gentile historians contemporary with the period (Polybius, for example) and latter-day Jewish historians (Josephus, for example), without citing evidence or giving their reasons, wrote of Alexander as an ignoble pretender to the throne. Perhaps these historians — cynical as this may sound — adopted their negative view of Alexander just because he was respectful of the Jews. Did these historians ask themselves, Why would any legitimate successor to the Syrian throne treat the Jews with honor and respect, and how could a man so noble be the true son of Antiochus Epiphanes? My work portrays Alexander as he is portrayed in First Maccabees and develops him in ways consistent with that portrayal.

THE TERMS *MACCABEES* AND *HASMONEANS*

The man known as *Maccabee* or *Judah Maccabee* or *Judah* or *Judah called Maccabee* or *Judas Maccabeus* is the central figure in the first and second books of Maccabees and also in my work. I have named my work for Maccabee because he provided the impetus for the first historical fight for religious liberty — even though the movement was begun by his father, Mattathias, and accomplished, however temporarily, by his brother Simon. I named my work for Maccabee also because he founded the holiday of Hanukah.

The term in the plural, *Maccabees*, does not appear in any of the books of Maccabees, nor does it appear in any other source of the period. Several centuries after

3

the events described in the books of Maccabees, Christians, admiring Judah Maccabee and his family, and considering the books of Maccabees sacred, and wanting to give a collective name to Judah, his father, his brothers, and other heroes of the period, pluralized the name in honor of Maccabee, the most famous hero of them all — hence, the books of Maccabees. The original titles of these books have been lost, except possibly for an unintelligible title to First Maccabees whose meaning is still being puzzled over by scholars.

Jews, recognizing that the name *Maccabee* belonged exclusively to Judah, preferred the collective term *Hasmoneans* for the entire family and its lineage. The name *Hasmoneans*, however, no less than *Maccabees*, is a name coined centuries after Maccabee and his brothers lived. Several possible origins for the term *Hasmoneans* have arisen, but the most famous is associated with the historian Josephus.

Josephus, writing in the first century C.E., two centuries after Mattathias and his sons lived, asserted that a man by the name of Asamonaios was Mattathias's great-grandfather (*Jewish Antiquities* XII: line 265, pp. 136–37). Josephus gives no source for this assertion and tells us nothing else about Asamonaios — and nothing else is known about him. But from the name *Asamonaios* came the collective name or term *Hasmoneans*. In Josephus's autobiography (*The Life*, pp. 1–4), Josephus states that he himself is the source of the information about the lineage of Asamonaios — and he implies that he is a highly reliable source at that — because, through his mother, he himself is descended from Asamonaios via the "daughter of Jonathan," one of the five sons of Mattathias. In other words, Josephus claims that he is descended from the same lineage as Mattathias, his sons, and the hereditary high priest descendants of that family, a lineage that Josephus calls "noble," even "royal."

Later generations of Jews expressed no skepticism of Josephus's distinguished lineage even though they considered Josephus a traitor because he went over to the side of the Romans during the Roman conquest of Judea in 70 C.E. Other curious origins for the term *Hasmoneans* exist but are beyond the scope of this introduction. Because the terms *Maccabees* and *Hasmoneans* originated much later than the events described, I have not included the terms in my work.

BACKGROUND: HELLENIZATION

In the fourth century B.C.E., Alexander the Great conquered a large part of the civilized world and imposed all things Greek upon it — Greek language, Greek culture, and Greek religion. This Greek-culture-based world became known as the hellenized world. Only the Jews — whether living in Judea or in the Diaspora — although not resisting hellenization as a whole, resisted the adoption of the Greek religion. Alexander the Great did not force the Greek religion upon the Jews, and neither did his immediate successors.

GREEK LANGUAGE

The Jews living in the hellenized world learned Greek along with Hebrew and Aramaic and were profoundly influenced by it.

Many Jews of the period had Greek names, such as Jason, Numenius [Noumenios], and Alcimus [Alkimos], just as today English-speaking Jews have English names. Some Jews had hellenized versions of Hebrew names, such as Mattathias, Jonas, Judas, and Jesus. Others had hybrid Greek and Hebrew names; for example, Jonathan Apphus, Eleazar Avaran, Jason ben Eleazar, Judah ben Calphi, Ptolemy ben Abubu, and Eupolemus, son of John ben Hakkoz.

The name for the land of Judah (originally named by the Hebrews for the tribe of Judah) was transliterated into Greek as *Ioudaia*. The Romans later latinized the Greek word into *Judea*, which meant in Latin what *Ioudaia* meant in Greek — "land of the Jews."

The word *synagogue*, so intimately associated with Jews, is Greek in origin. It comes from the Greek word *sunagoge*, which originally had no association with Jews at all. The primary meaning of *sunagoge* was a "uniting" or "bringing together." By extension, and with the passage of time, *sunagoge* came to mean a "group" or "collection" or "gathering." Originally the collection could have been fruit as well as people, but with the continued passage of time, *sunagoge* came to mean primarily a collection of people. The collection could be of various sizes, and the specific size had to be determined by the reader from the context; thus, *sunagoge* has been variously translated as "group," "collection," "gathering," "band," "company," "delegation," "congregation," "assembly," or "convention."

By the time *sunagoge* was associated exclusively with people, the word had developed a secondary meaning — an extension of the first — which was a "meeting place." The meeting place did not necessarily have a physical structure, and the group of people meeting were still not necessarily Jews. Even when they were Jews, however, as in the first book of Maccabees, there was no implication that there was a structure specifically designed for the meeting or that the primary intent of the meeting was for worship or study.

The noun *sunagoge* appears four times in First Maccabees. Each time it describes a gathering of Jews, and each time a different purpose is given for the gathering. In only one case (number 2 below) is that gathering even partially for religious reasons. In no case is a physical structure described or implied.

1. "A *group* [*sunagoge*] of Hasids came together . . . for the purpose of joining Mattathias" (1 Macc 2:42). These Hasids joined Mattathias to be part of the resistance movement.

2. "A *gathering* [*sunagoge*] came together to prepare for war and pray" (1 Macc 3:44). In this case the context indicates that the young men of Israel gathered primarily to join Maccabee to fight. The warriors prayed for mercy and compassion but especially for victory. In the first and second books of Maccabees, Jewish warriors pray frequently — not in buildings but on the battlefield.

3. "A *delegation* [*sunagoge*] of scribes appeared [before the enemy] for the purpose of obtaining justice" (1 Macc 7:12). The delegation came to negotiate with the enemy.

4. "These writings were read before a great *assembly* [*sunagoge*] of priests, people, leaders, and elders" (1 Macc 14:28). This was a large gathering that met for

the purpose of reading aloud tributes to Simon from the gentile nations. After hearing the tributes, the Jewish people honored Simon and memorialized his family.

These examples show the state of the evolution of the word *sunagoge* in Judea at the time of Maccabee and his brothers, when the Temple in Jerusalem was the sole house of worship (and not only sacrifice), and the priests, and to a much lesser extent the elders, were the sole religious leaders. Throughout the books of Maccabees, references to the Temple and the priests are frequent, but there are no references to synagogues or rabbis.

It is not known when *sunagoge* came to mean a building for the purpose of worship or study or when such a building was exclusively for Jews. George Foot Moore writes, "There is indeed no mention of synagogues at all in Jewish writings surviving from the centuries preceding the Christian era" (Vol. 1, p. 285). Although the Mishnah refers to a time when there was a synagogue as a building in close proximity to the Temple (Yoma 7:1; Sotah 7:7), the Mishnah does not define the time; therefore, we cannot assume that this special synagogue existed before the first century C.E.

The first datable mention of synagogues as houses of worship or study for Jews in Judea occurs in New Testament writings that describe events of the first century C.E. — in the Gospels (for example, Luke 4:44; John 18:20) and in the Acts of the Apostles (for example, 24:11–12). Similarly, the first mention of the title *rabbi*, so intimately linked with synagogues, occurs in these same writings. The *Encyclopaedia Judaica* entry for *rabbi* (Vol. 13, p. 1445) comments that the context in which the word *rabbi* is used in Matthew 23:1–7 indicates the "recent introduction" of this title.

In the Diaspora, synagogues as houses of worship or study for Jews appear to have been well established by the first century C.E. Paul reports them in nearly all the major cities of his travels "among all the Jews throughout the world" (Acts 24:5), including Athens (Acts 17:16–17). This suggests that synagogues may have existed before the first century in the Diaspora, but exactly when such buildings arose is not known. (See Moore, Vol. 1, pp. 281–88 and note 52, pp. 88–90.)

The word *sunagoge* shows the profound influence of hellenization and the Greek language on the Jewish people, for we have in *synagogue* a remarkable example of a Greek-based word that names Judaism's most cherished, important, and influential institution.

Ecclesia is a Greek word originally meaning "assembly" or "congregation." In ancient Athens, it meant a "political assembly." In Judea, *ecclesia* came to mean a meeting place, synonymous with *sunagoge*. The first book of Maccabees reports that "Judah Maccabee and his brothers and the whole *congregation* [*ecclesia*] of Israel ordained that the Festival of Dedication should be celebrated for eight days at this season every year" (1 Macc 4:59). One may be surprised to see the word *ecclesia* here instead of the word *sunagoge* because people today associate *ecclesia* exclusively with the Christian church. At the time of Judah Maccabee, however, the church had not yet come into being. The split in meaning between the two words *sunagoge* and *ecclesia* came only after the split of Christianity from its mother religion Judaism, late in the first or early in the second

9

century C.E.   At that time the two words assumed their meaning of a religious meeting place or congregation, with or without edifice: *synagogue* for Jews, and *ecclesia* for Christians.

Bima is a Greek word meaning "a raised place to speak from in public assembly." Notice that the ancient word had no religious significance and was not associated with the Jews or with a religious building.

Of Greek origin, too, are the words *Genesis*, *Exodus*, *Leviticus*, *Deuteronomy*, and *Apocrypha*.

Although Jews in Judea spoke and read Hebrew in the Temple, and wrote some of their secular and semi-secular books in Hebrew (for example, the original first book of Maccabees), Jews wrote a large body of secular and semi-secular literature in Greek (for example, the second, third, and fourth books of Maccabees). The most famous Jewish philosopher in antiquity, Philo, wrote his works in Greek, as did Josephus, the most famous Jewish historian in antiquity. Josephus relates that in the third century B.C.E., an Egyptian king requested Judean Jews to translate the Hebrew Scriptures into Greek because he wanted a copy in Greek for his library in Alexandria (*Jewish Antiquities* XII: lines 86–109, pp. 43–55).   This translation became known as the *Septuagint*, a word of Latin origin meaning *seventy*, because supposedly seventy Jewish scholars did the translation. Modern writers of the history of religion (for example, Moore, Vol. 1, p. 288) relate that the Septuagint was created not so much to please the Egyptian king as to benefit the Alexandrian Jewish community, who wanted to understand the Scriptures in their native language — Greek.

Because the Septuagint, apart from its many puzzles, is a translation of the Hebrew Scriptures, Jews do not consider the Septuagint sacred any more than they consider the King James translation, however majestic and poetic, to be sacred. Jews, and others as well, know how often information gets lost, not to mention distorted and adulterated and even mutilated, in translation. As an example of this, the name of God will be discussed shortly.

GREEK CULTURE AND RELIGION

In addition to the Greek language, Jews, particularly educated and wealthy ones, adopted much Greek culture, including the love of sports and, we may presume — for it is difficult to imagine otherwise — the love of art, theater, and literature.

But the Jews as a whole, even those who enjoyed Greek culture, refused to convert to the Greek religion. There is no evidence that any of the Hellenic leaders in Judea made an issue of conversion for the Jews until the advent of Antiochus Epiphanes. Alexander the Great had been tolerant and hitherto apparently had set a good example.

Jews resisted conversion to the Greek religion for several reasons. They cherished their own religion, based as it was upon a belief in the existence of the one eternal God, Creator of all humanity, whose teachings (the Torah) had been revealed to Moses on Mount Sinai. The Jews believed, too, that these teachings assured them an ethical, meaningful, and satisfying life, with the hope — for those who wished to hold this belief — of a hereafter.

Moreover, the Jews found three elements of the Greek religion particularly abhorrent:

First and foremost, polytheism not only conflicted with their belief in the one God, but intellectually and philosophically it was neither economical nor cohesive.

Second, in Hebrew theology, the Creator made the universe. In Greek theology, the universe made the gods. Zeus is clearly not just another name for the God of the Hebrews. (The religion of Olympian Zeus figures prominently in First Maccabees.)

Third, the mystery cult surrounding Dionysus, son of Zeus, was particularly distasteful to the Jews. Dionysus was the god of the vine, and his celebration took place with the drinking of wine, which his celebrants believed resulted in union with the god. Moreover, initiates in the cult believed that they alone, because they were believers in Dionysus, were assured of eternal life. Many Jews (like many Greeks, particularly the philosophers) already believed in the immortality of the soul, and the Jews associated immortality with good deeds, not with a belief in God. (Among the Jews, the concept of the resurrection of the body was in its infancy at the time of Judah Maccabee.) According to the Hebrew prophet Isaiah, the Hebrew God did not require a belief in him to assure his favor, as the case of Cyrus the Great illustrates; what God required was to do his will. (The cult of Dionysus figures prominently in the third book of Maccabees; an illuminating account of it may be found in Euripides' play *Bacchae*.)

In the second century B.C.E., Antiochus Epiphanes of Syria insisted that the Greek religion become the universal religion of his realm, which included Judea. Antiochus demanded that the Jews convert or be killed. Many Jews understandably converted. A converted Jew, no less than a gentile, was obliged to betray, persecute, and kill faithful Jews, and many converted Jews went about their task with great zeal. First Maccabees reports that some converts "did evil . . . to the children of Israel surpassing that done by the gentiles" (1 Macc 7:23).

LETTERS, DOCUMENTS, AND QUOTATIONS

Because scholars consider most of the letters and proclamations in the books of Maccabees to be copies of authentic historical documents, I have translated them faithfully, although sometimes in abridged form. These texts may readily be recognized by their indentation and smaller-sized print, with omitted parts indicated by ellipses.

All other quotations in my work are either dialogue I created for the characters or are my own translations of the source texts. References for the quoted passages from source texts are provided on pages 407–412.

DATES

The dates in *Maccabee* follow those in First Maccabees because that book is considered the most historical of the four. These dates are given in accordance with what was then called the Era of the Kingdom of the Greeks, or the Seleucid Era.

After Alexander the Great died, his empire was divided among his favorite generals. After the division, the empire consisted of three major kingdoms: Macedonia and Greece, Egypt, and Syria and Babylon. The empire also included many provinces ruled by the three kingdoms. Among these provinces were Cilicia, Phoenicia, Coele-Syria, and — most important from the standpoint of the books of Maccabees — Judea. At the time of Judah Maccabee, Judea was ruled for the most part by Syria (as in First and Second Maccabees) and infrequently by Egypt (as in Third Maccabees).

Seleucus I was the first of Alexander's beneficiaries to assume a throne. He was crowned king of Syria, thereby launching the Seleucid Era, also called — more importantly from the standpoint of the books of Maccabees — the Era of the Kingdom of the Greeks. Seleucus assumed the throne in the first year of the Era of the Kingdom of the Greeks; this corresponds in modern reckoning to 312 or 311 B.C.E.

The existence of a one-year discrepancy between the various historical works of the period ought not be surprising. A one-year variation for antiquity is actually a remarkably small error — disconcerting perhaps to historians but not to mathematicians and statisticians.

To convert dates from the Seleucid calendar to the modern one B.C.E., we begin with 312 (or 311) and subtract the Seleucid date from it. For example, Mattathias died, according to the Seleucid calendar, in the 146th year of the Kingdom of the Greeks. $312 - 146 = 166$. Thus, Mattathias died in 166 B.C.E. (or 165 B.C.E. if one begins with 311). Maccabee died in the 152nd year of the Kingdom of the Greeks. $312 - 152 = 160$. Thus, Maccabee died in 160 B.C.E. To promote ease of following the time flow, I have in-

14

cluded the B.C.E. dates of the most important events in brackets in the table of contents and also in the corresponding places in the story.

TOWNS AND CITIES

When an ancient town or city has a modern name or a famous one, I chose the modern or famous name out of consideration for the modern reader, even when doing so was anachronistic; for example, I chose Acre over Ptolemais, Jaffa over Joppa, and Ashdod over Azotus. When describing ancient towns or cities that have not been located or for which no modern or famous name exists, I used the ancient name as given in the books of Maccabees; for example, Dathema, Bascama, and Maspha.

HANUKAH
INAUGURATION OF THE HOLIDAY

In addition to their general historical interest, the first and second books of Maccabees are particularly important because they tell the story of the first Hanukah, the Festival of Dedication, which was inaugurated by Judah Maccabee. These two books tell us that Hanukah commemorates two events:

1. the dedication (or rededication) of the Temple after it was purified and restored from its pollution and desecration by the gentiles: "Let us go up [to the Temple Mount] to cleanse and dedicate [*enkainisai*] the Temple" (1 Macc 4:36);

2. the dedication of the new altar of burnt offerings in the Temple: "On the twenty-fifth day of Kislev . . . they . . . offered sacrifice . . . upon the new altar of burnt offerings. . . . [The altar] was dedicated [*enekain-isthe*] with songs" (1 Macc 4:52–54).

When Judah Maccabee first announced his intentions, his plans were only to cleanse and dedicate the Temple (see item 1 above). He apparently originally intended only to cleanse the altar along with the rest of the Temple. Later Maccabee decided not to cleanse the altar but to destroy it and build a new one (1 Macc 4:44–46).

The books of Maccabees do not tell us why Judah decided to destroy the altar, but it is reasonable to surmise that the stones were so severely stained they could not be cleaned. Moreover, the stains were the blood of pigs. He must have thought he had no choice but to destroy the altar. Having destroyed the altar and built a new one, Maccabee decided on the additional ceremony to dedicate the new altar (see item 2 above).

However, the stones from the wrecked old altar presented a problem: like the Temple itself, the old altar was sacred, however polluted. It was built by Cyrus the Great, king of the Persians and Medes, at the command of God. Cyrus was a very important righteous gentile in the history of the Hebrews. (Pharaoh's daughter, who adopted and raised Moses, and Jethro, Moses' father-in-law, were two others.) Cyrus, in Isaiah's amazing words which he attributes to God, was God's "shepherd" and "my anointed." In the sixth century B.C.E., Cyrus freed the Jews from their Babylonian captivity and led them back to Jerusalem. Cyrus, who did not even know God, let alone believe in him, was then told by God to rebuild Jerusalem and lay the foundation of the Temple:

> Thus says YHV, your Redeemer. . . who says of Cyrus, "He is my shepherd, and he shall fulfill all my purpose"; saying of Jerusalem, "She shall be built," and of the temple, "Your foundation shall be laid" (Isa 44:24–28).

> Thus says YHV to his anointed, to Cyrus [rendered in the Vulgate as *christo meo Cyro*, which means "to my christ, to Cyrus"], "whose right hand I have held to subdue nations: . . . it is I, YHV, the God of Israel, who call you by your name [*Cyrus*]. For the sake of my servant Jacob, and Israel my chosen, I call you by your name [*Cyrus*], I surname you [*my anointed, my messiah*, or *my christ* — all three words are synonymous], though you do not know me" (Isa 45:1–4).

Isaiah's prophecy, let alone his choice of words, was stunning. The prophecy largely came true: Although Cyrus did not live to see the rebuilding of the Temple, he designated funds for that purpose. His successors, Darius and Artaxerxes, also gentile kings of Persia, carried out Cyrus's wishes — *God's wishes* — and provided the funds, although Zerubbabel and other Hebrews or their designees did the actual construction (Ezra 3:2; 3:6–9).

Jews have been reluctant to give Cyrus and his successors credit, let alone to call Cyrus God's "shepherd" and "anointed" or "messiah." Christians have been equally reluctant to call Cyrus God's "christ." As a result, although Isaiah may be the most frequently quoted of the Hebrew prophets, this important passage tends to be ignored.

Judah Maccabee may have initially ignored this passage, too, for in destroying the altar, Maccabee destroyed a part of the Temple, which was built at the direction of Cyrus by the command of God. No sooner had Maccabee destroyed the altar, however, than he must have realized his possible error, for he ordered that the altar stones not be discarded like trash, like some of the other polluted but ordinary stones, but be saved in a special place on the Temple Mount "until such time as a prophet would come and tell them what to do with them" (1 Macc 4:46).

RITUAL

Some of the standard elements of the holiday of Sukkot, which had not been celebrated in the Temple for three years, were incorporated into the celebration of that first Hanukah (2 Macc 10:6–8). One major element of the Temple celebration of Sukkot was the libation ceremony, which included the illumination of the Temple courts with colossal lamps. The Mishnah tells us that in the celebration of Sukkot, so many lamps and so much oil was used, and the light was so bright, that "there was not a courtyard in Jerusalem that did not reflect the light" (Danby, pp. 179–80).

I have based my reconstruction of the first Hanukah largely on the illumination component of the libation ceremony in Sukkot because in a short time illumination became the dominant feature of the Hanukah celebration. Although great illumination took place only on the first night of Sukkot, such illumination took place on all eight nights of Hanukah. In time, the illumination ceremony disappeared from Sukkot, appropriated by Hanukah. So impressive and so important was illumination in the Hanukah celebration that two centuries after the inauguration of the new holiday, Josephus referred to the festival not as Hanukah (*Enkainia* in Greek), the Festival of Dedication, but as *Phota* (in Greek), the Festival of Lights (*Jewish Antiquities* XII: line 325, pp. 168–69). Josephus was the only extant ancient source to call the holiday by this name.

The New Testament, some parts apparently written contemporarily with the works of Josephus, refers to the festival by its original name of Hanukah, *Enkainia* in Greek, the Festival of Dedication (John 10:22), and that name has remained the holiday's primary name, even in places where it has taken the secondary name of Festival of Lights, or *Hag ha-Urim* in Hebrew (Goodman, *The Hanukkah Anthology*, p. 277).

In my reconstruction of the first Hanukah, in addition to the illumination ceremony, I also incorporated another major element from the ancient celebration of Sukkot: namely, the recitation of the Hallel — Psalms 113–118. (For more about the ancient celebrations of Sukkot and Hanukah, I suggest Moore, Vol. 2, pp. 43–51.)

There is no evidence in any of the historical accounts of a shortage of pure oil during the celebration of that first Hanukah. Quite the contrary. And the legend of a single cruse of oil that miraculously burned for eight days appeared for the first time in the Middle Ages in the medieval *Scholia* in *Megillat Taanit* 9. This account was later incorporated almost verbatim into the Talmud, tractate *Shabbat 21b* (Goodman, pp. 33, 50, 71).

Lighting the lamps of the seven-branched lampstand within the Temple alone would have required more than a single cruse of oil. But that first Hanukah was celebrated in the manner of Sukkot, which required not only the lighting of the sanctuary lampstand but also the lighting of the colossal lamps in the Temple courtyards, each of which held many gallons of oil.

Moreover, the legend of the single cruse of oil has always seemed to me not only to minimize what Maccabee and his brothers accomplished, but also to trivialize — rather than magnify — the power of God. After all, we are talking about the God who created the universe and everything in it. I am not alone in this evaluation. See the poems "Meditation on Hanukkah" by Charles Reznikoff and "The Miracle" by Philip M. Raskin (Goodman, pp. 217–18; 365–66). But especially see the Talmud itself, tract *Or Zarua* 1.139[8], which says that God told Moses to tell Aaron: "[The] offerings to the sanctuary shall be employed only so long as [the Temple] endures, but the lights of the Hanukah festival will shine forever" (Goodman, p. 78).

Psalm 118, too, much more effectively than the legend of the small cruse of oil, proclaims the power of God: "This is the day which YHV has made" (Ps 118:24) and "God is YHV, who has given us light" (Ps 118:27).

Although First Maccabees gives primacy to Judah Maccabee for the inauguration of Hanukah, it also credits his brothers, and the whole congregation of Israel, for determining three important features regarding the celebration of the holiday: that Hanukah should be celebrated (1) commencing on the twenty-fifth day of Kislev, (2) for eight days, and (3) in a joyous mood. "Maccabee and his brothers and the whole congregation of Israel ordained that the Festival of Dedication should be celebrated for eight days at this season every year, beginning the twenty-fifth day of Kislev. And the festival was to be kept with joy and gladness" (1 Macc 4:59).

THE ANGLICIZATION OF *HANUKAH*

Because *Maccabee* is written in English, I spell and pronounce the word *Hanukah* in its Anglicized form, with a voiced *h* as in the name *Hannah* or the word *Hasid*. Anglicization simplifies and standardizes spelling, adapts a foreign word to the English language, and facilitates its becoming part of English, all of which enhance communication. Anglicization long ago occurred with the words *Sabbath*, *Isaiah*, *Jerusalem*, *Israel*, *Isaac*, *Zion*, and others — all without variation, without self-consciousness, without controversy.

Hebraists who choose to pronounce the name of the holiday with a guttural *h* in English do not need the spelling *ch* to do so. However, *ch* presents a stumbling block to the non-Hebraist because the English rules of spelling and phonics dictate that *ch* followed by the vowel *a* must be pronounced as in the word *channel*, a sound that yields the wrong results.

Some people prefer the spelling *Chanukah* because it makes the name of the holiday look more like the word

21

Christmas, but such attachment is unreasonable because Hanukah is not "Jewish Christmas" and *ch* does not make it so; it only creates further confusion.

Discussing the other variant spellings of Hanukah is beyond the scope of this introduction. To learn more about the linguistic analysis of the word *Hanukah*, I suggest two sources: the Philologos article "On Language: A Hanukah Gift to My Editors" (*Forward* [weekly Jewish newspaper, New York] 19 Dec. 2003, p. 11) and *Happy Hanukah: A Music Book to Celebrate the Festival of Dedication* by Judith S. Rubenstein (El Cajon, CA: Granite Hills Press, 2003, p. vii).

THE THIRD BOOK OF MACCABEES

The third book of Maccabees is the most controversial of the four books. William Fairweather's 1926 statement remains the most succinct summary of the controversy: "The third book of Maccabees, although purporting to be an historical narrative, is really an animated . . . piece of fiction. . . . Possibly, however, the story may be founded on some historical situation regarding which we have no definite knowledge" (*Encyclopaedia Britannica*, Vol. 17, p. 199). In other words, maybe Third Maccabees is fiction — and maybe it isn't.

Egyptian Jews did not deny the authenticity of Third Maccabees. In fact, until modern times, Egyptian Jews celebrated a holiday commemorating the events of the third book, just as the rest of Jewry has celebrated the holiday of Purim, which commemorates events from the book of Esther, now considered by most scholars to be a work of fiction. Although the stories have a certain similarity, the differences between the Purim story and the Egyptian one are marked:

In Purim, the villain is Haman, a gentile who is the prime minister of Persia. He issues a death decree for all of Persia's Jews. The hero is Esther, a Jew who is the gentile king's wife and queen. Esther, with the help of her Jewish uncle Mordecai, and with the full support of the gentile king Ahasuerus, her husband, prevents Haman's decree from going into effect.

In the Egyptian story, the sole driving force is the gentile king of Egypt, Ptolemy Philopator, apparently a great soldier on the field, but on the throne an alcoholic with episodes of confusion and paranoid delusions. It is the king himself who issues the death decree for the Egyptian Jews, and it is the king himself who rescinds that decree. There is no Jewish hero. Neither is there a gentile of power and influence who manipulates the king. Although the king has a servant named Hermon, Hermon has no power and does not manipulate the king. Some people may find the names Hermon and Haman similar, but any similarity between the names is coincidental, and there are no similarities between the two men.

In the Egyptian story, the king begins as villain and ends as hero — unless it is the God of Israel who is the real hero. God's presence is felt in the story, unlike in the Purim story where God is significantly absent. The Egyptian story is clearly very different from the Persian or the Purim story.

Many of the events related in Third Maccabees are similar to those of the Holocaust, and for this reason I think it is unreasonable to dismiss the third book as a work of fiction. The common theme of all four books of Maccabees (and also the book of Esther) is the intent of some powerful gentiles to annihilate the Jews — and the survival of the Jews in spite of this intent. This theme, unfortunately, has been universally true for so long that it hardly seems to matter whether every detail of the stories is historical.

THE FOURTH BOOK OF MACCABEES

Fourth Maccabees is a philosophical treatise ostensibly in praise of reason over emotion but more obviously in praise of martyrdom. Martyrdom is the deliberate choice to die for one's beliefs rather than to live by forsaking them. Martyrdom figures significantly in the books of Maccabees, but particularly in the fourth book.

In Fourth Maccabees, Antiochus Epiphanes forces an old priest and a mother and her seven sons to eat pork and live, or to die by torture. The martyrs refuse to violate their religion, and they suffer the consequences. An abbreviated variant of the same story, without religious philosophy, is told in Second Maccabees (6:18–7:42). Drawing on both versions, I have told the story without praising martyrdom.

Some people praise martyrdom while others do not, perhaps considering it ultimately and in fact a form of suicide. The Torah teaches, in the matter of choosing between life and death, to choose life (Deut 30:19). Without citing Torah, Mattathias chooses life in First Maccabees when deciding whether Jews should keep the Sabbath or defend themselves when attacked. Mattathias says, "If we all . . . refuse to fight for our lives on the

Sabbath, we shall soon be rooted out of the earth"
(1 Macc 2:40).

Whether one favors martyrdom or not, nothing di-
minishes the nobility and sincerity of the martyrs of this
story — the old priest and the woman and her seven
sons. Their speeches and behavior are unequaled in religious literature. Even Antiochus Epiphanes, who orders
and supervises their torture and death, cannot help admiring them. The Roman Catholic Church has made
saints of the mother and her sons — and has canonized
and made part of its sacred Bible the first two books of
Maccabees but not the last two.

Incidentally, the names of the mother and her seven
sons are not given in the books of Maccabees. Not until
the sixteenth century did a Spanish Catholic editor give
the mother the name of Hannah, by which name she has
become famous, even among Jews. She remains un-
named in my work.

SPECIAL CHALLENGES OF TRANSLATION
NAMES OF THE DEITY

In First Maccabees, the author scrupulously avoids
referring to the Deity by name. Instead he uses circum-
locutions, ellipses, the vague word *Heaven,* and rarely
the word *Lord* [*Kurios*, in the Greek]. This avoidance
provides evidence that the author of First Maccabees
was a Jew. Moreover, the style of the book is reminis-
cent of the Hebrew Scriptures, further evidence that the
author was a Jew.

The author of Second Maccabees, presumed by scholars also to be a Jew, likewise avoids calling the Deity by name. But in addition to the word *Lord* (*Kurie*, 2 Macc 1:24), the author readily uses the word *God* (*Ho Theos,* 2 Macc 1:2), and occasionally such phrases as *Almighty God* (*Pantokratoros Theos,* 2 Macc 3:22) and *Lord God* (*Kurie Ho Theos,* 2 Macc 1:24).

Like the author of Second Maccabees, many Jews today, myself included, are comfortable thinking, writing, and speaking about God with the word *God,* even though that word is derived from ancient heathen theology. *Theos* in Greek and *Deus* in Latin are likewise derived from heathen theology — specifically from the name of Zeus, the greatest of the Greek gods.

The word *God* has different meanings for different religions and different people, so a definition is in order. Whenever I use the word, I mean the God of all humanity in accordance with the Hebrew definition given in the first chapters of Genesis. I also use the words *Creator* and *Almighty* as synonyms for *God.*

Whenever I quote a passage from the Hebrew Scriptures containing the ineffable name of God, I have partially transliterated the name as YHV — an unpronounceable symbol. Because Jews are forbidden to say the name of God aloud, a substitute word is required.

For millennia, Jews speaking Hebrew (and writing secular works in Hebrew) have frequently used the substitute word *Adonai,* perhaps because that word sometimes appears in Hebrew Scriptures as a title for God — not his name — such as Adonai God. Greek Jews have used the Greek word *Kurios* (see the previous examples from First and Second Maccabees), and Roman Jews have used the Latin word *Dominus*. All three of these words mean "Lord." Since the advent of the English language in relatively recent times, English-speaking Jews have in fact used the word *Lord*. For example, the first commandment is usually translated from Hebrew as "I am the Lord your God" (Exod 20:2).

The first commandment is a good example of why I have deliberately chosen not to use *Adonai*, *Kurios*, *Dominus*, or *Lord* as a substitute word for the ineffable name of God. The word *Lord* in any language has created — and continues to create — confusion, mainly because over time many people seem to have forgotten that *Lord* is a substitute word for the ineffable name of God — YHV. To prevent confusion and ambiguity, were I to translate the first commandment, I would do so thus: "I am YHV your God."

The word *Lord*, in addition to being a substitute word for the name of God, has become a theological term and a synonym for God, which only adds to the confusion. Since antiquity, the word *Lord* has been used also as a term of respect for any man and as a sociological or political title for a distinguished man. Confusion reigns when the word *Lord* does not of itself indicate whether God or a respected man is being referred to. Moreover, the word *Lord* has gender: it is exclusively male. By contrast, the name of God is without gender, is not a sociological or political title, and is not a term of respect for a man. It is simply a proper name — and, to Jews, the most important name of all. Finally, and most to the point, the Hebrew Scriptures do not use *Adonai* or *Lord* when the name of God is intended; the

27

Scriptures use the name of God.

For these reasons, I have not used the word *Lord* in those places where God's name appears in Hebrew Scriptures. Instead, I have used the symbol *YHV*, as I did in the above example of the first commandment. The symbol *YHV* plainly shows where the name of God appears in the Hebrew Scriptures, whereas the word *Lord* disguises it, even if the disguise is unintended.

When I am reading the Scriptures aloud and the name of God appears in the text, I personally substitute the word *God* or *Creator* or *Almighty*. For those who prefer a Hebrew word, I suggest *HaShem* (which means "The Name"), a phrase coined by Orthodox Jews that states in the most straightforward manner that the articulated phrase is a substitute for the name of God — YHV.

TORAH AND NOMOS

In the books of Maccabees, the Greek word *nomos* may present problems to the translator. *Nomos* is conventionally translated as "law." However, such a translation in most contexts of the books of Maccabees is misleading and in fact erroneous. *Nomos* is generally used in the books of Maccabees to mean the Torah, the first five books of the Hebrew Bible (the Pentateuch), sacred to Jews and Christians and, according to the Koran, to Muslims as well. (See Al-ahqaf 46:12; Jonah 10:90–93; Story 28:2–6; Night Journey 17:103; Cow 2:40–58, 2:174, 2:210; Women 4:98–100; Table 5:20, 5:44, 5:48; and other verses in the Koran.)

The Torah contains many teachings pertaining to religious observances or laws: the teaching of the Covenant

and the teaching of all the commandments, including the
Ten Commandments, the dietary commandments, the
sacrificial ones, the ethical ones, and even some that are
inexplicable. These teachings collectively may be considered "the law."

But the Torah also contains the teaching of stories —
those of creation, of early mankind, and of primitive Judaism. These stories, often without providing answers
to the questions they generate, lend themselves to endless discussions, many of a moral or ethical nature. A
few evoke only puzzlement.

It should be clear that the word *law* is much too re-
strictive to apply to the entire compendium of teachings
called the Torah. Consequently, I have usually translated *nomos* as "the Torah" or "the teaching(s)" or "the
teaching of the Creator" or an equivalent phrase that con-
veys its actual meaning. I have only rarely translated it
as "law" or "religious law," and only in cases that refer
strictly to the commandments or in situations where people are using the word *law* to ridicule the religion of the
Jews — a not uncommon use of the word.

Most scholars believe that First Maccabees was originally written in Hebrew. I suggest that in its original
Hebrew the author in fact used the word *Torah* wherever
nomos appears in the translated Greek.

It should not be necessary to point out that the law is
honorable and noble, and no society could survive without it. Civil and religious laws, however primitive,
were designed to benefit men and prevent them from
succumbing to no law at all, to natural law, or to the law
of self-interest or the jungle. Anyone who thinks good
behavior comes about naturally or exists already in

men's hearts is a supreme idealist with little understanding of the human heart. Nonetheless, the word *law*, as I have already said, has acquired a pejorative meaning, especially when applied to the religion of the Jews. Such disparagement is dispelled when one translates the word *Torah* by its authentic meaning of "teaching."

Incidentally, although Liddell and Scott's *Greek-English Lexicon* gives as the meaning of *anomos* "lawless" or "without law," and although this meaning is literally correct, it is nonetheless misleading and erroneous in the context of the books of Maccabees, where *anomos* specifically means "without Torah." It does not mean "lawless" in the sense of outlaws or bandits. *Anomos* only describes Jewish converts to the Greek religion — apostates from Judaism or Jews *without Torah*. It is not used to describe Mattathias or his sons or their followers, who might well have been considered *lawless* or *outlaws* from the Greek perspective.

COVER PICTURE

There are no extant paintings or sculptures from the period of Maccabee and his brothers, and probably none ever existed. Jewish art depicting people is almost nonexistent in antiquity, largely because of the second of the Ten Commandments. Moreover, gentile artists prior to the first century C.E. had little or no interest in portraying Jewish subjects or themes.

First Maccabees tells us that Judah Maccabee wore armor and brandished a sword, and that as a warrior "he looked like a giant" (1 Macc 3:3). None of the books tells whether he ever rode a horse, but some Jews of the time rode horses into battle, according to the author of First Maccabees (1 Macc 16:4).

The cover picture is based upon a medieval manuscript illumination by an unknown French Christian artist of the thirteenth century C.E. The original is in the collection of the Pierpont Morgan Library, New York. The picture depicts an ancient battle scene in which the Hebrews are victorious. Although the original painting does not specifically represent Judah Maccabee and his brothers, it does represent ancient Hebrew warriors in a moment of victory. Curiously, the painting shows the Hebrews wearing hammerhead helmets. One of the possible origins of the name *Maccabee* is the Hebrew word *maccabee*, which means "hammer." Perhaps the "hammer" meaning of *Maccabee* was known by Christians of medieval times, and the French artist was under the impression that a hammerhead helmet was characteristic of Jewish warrior-heroes of any period.

I suggested to the cover artist that he base his design upon that painting in spite of its many anachronisms because, to my knowledge, it is one of the oldest extant works of art depicting an ancient Hebrew battle scene in which the Jews are victorious — and are wearing hammerhead helmets.

THE SIGNIFICANCE OF HANUKAH
AND OF THE SECOND CENTURY B.C.E. JEWISH WARS

The campaigns waged by Maccabee and his brothers on behalf of the Jews were at first wars for religious liberty and survival as a people; later they were also for the independence of the Jewish nation. However, the significance of these wars goes far beyond the history of the Jews.

These campaigns constitute the first recorded war for religious liberty. The war was fundamentally a fight for respect for differences between peoples, for human rights, for social justice, and for human dignity. It was a fight of resistance to the intolerant, who insist that their religion is the only true one and is therefore deserving of universality.

At great cost over the course of more than thirty years, Maccabee and his brothers fought and finally won their war, however temporarily. Had this war not been won, the Jews and Judaism, with its central tenet of monotheism, would not have survived; and Christianity and Islam, at least as we know them, would not have come into being. These wars, therefore, deeply shaped the course of Western civilization — and continue to shape it.

The fight for religious liberty did not end with Maccabee and his brothers. Throughout history, tyrants have forced their "true" and "universal" religions upon others, and they continue to do so. Unfortunately, countless millions have perished during the struggle. Fortunately for civilization, a valiant few have always been willing to fight the intolerant majority to preserve the liberty of all.

MACCABEE

PROLOGUE

Alexander the Great

And it came to pass
that Alexander,
the son of Philip of Macedon,
marched to the ends of the earth,
conquering and plundering as he went
and imposing all things Greek
upon the conquered peoples.

Alexander waged many wars,
conquered many nations,
and slew many kings.

After conquering Thebes,
he united it with all
the other Greek city-states.
Then he crossed the Hellespont
and conquered Halicarnassus
and liberated the other Greek cities
that had been taken by the Persians.

Then he conquered Syria
and marched south,
capturing Phoenicia and Tyre,

Judea and Jerusalem,
and Philistia and Gaza.
And he marched on to Egypt
and captured it, too,
and founded Alexandria,
a city named for him.

Then Alexander marched back
through Philistia, Judea, and Phoenicia
to conquer Persia.
And after Babylon fell,
he marched over the mountains
and captured Media,
the land of the Medes,
and went all the way to India.

After he killed Darius,
the king of the Persians and Medes,
Alexander ruled as king
over all of Greece—
the first man to do so.
And everywhere Alexander went
that place became Greek—
adopting Greek customs and ways,
speaking the Greek language,
and worshiping the Greek gods.

He assembled mighty armies
to rule over many nations
and many provinces.
And the kings of those places
paid tribute to him.

He made Babylon
the capital of his empire,
and the whole earth was at peace.

Alexander was proud
of his accomplishments.
He was greatly exalted
because of them,
and the whole world called him
Alexander the Great.

Alexander ruled and conquered
for only twelve years.
Then suddenly,
at Babylon,
he fell ill and lay dying.

He called his men
to his deathbed.
The doors to his palace
were thrown wide open,
and countless weeping soldiers
filed past their dying commander.
He divided his kingdom
among his generals—
friends from his youth—
and then Alexander the Great died.

The Founding of the Kingdom of the Greeks

Seleucus, one of Alexander's generals
and dearest friends,
became king of Babylon and Syria
and the provinces round about them.
Cassander inherited Macedon and Greece.
Ptolemy inherited Egypt.
All these kingdoms together
were now called the Kingdom of the Greeks.

Seleucus was the first
to place a crown upon his head,
and in his honor,
the first year of his reign was called
the first year of the Seleucid era—
the first year
of the Kingdom of the Greeks.   [312 B.C.E.]

Soon
the several kings
were quarreling among themselves
and fighting
and going to war.
And the peace
won so proudly
by Alexander
disappeared from the face of the earth.

PROLOGUE

The crossroads of the marching armies
was the tiny province of Judea,
whose paths and fields were trampled
by soldiers and horses
and were rutted by chariot wheels.
Judea and her people suffered greatly
because of the countless intruders.

As each warring king died,
his son placed the crown
upon his head,
as did his son after him.
And evil multiplied upon the earth.

BALLAD 1
ANTIOCHUS EPIPHANES

Antiochus "Light of the World"

There came forth
from the sons of Seleucus
the most evil shoot of all.
His name was Antiochus Epiphanes.

As soon as his father died,
Antiochus became king.
All the people bowed down before him
and kissed his feet,
as if he were a god.
So he took the name Epiphanes,
which means "shining like the dawn"
or like a great beacon,
or like the divine light
that emanates from a Greek god
who comes down from heaven
and walks among men upon the earth.
Antiochus Epiphanes—
Antiochus "God Manifest to Men,"
Antiochus "Light of the World."

Antiochus Epiphanes
came to power in the 137th year
of the Kingdom of the Greeks.   [175 B.C.E.]
He was king of Syria
and all its provinces,
including Judea,
the land of the Jews,
the children of Israel.

A Clash of Cultures

In those days
there were within Judea
highly persuasive men,
men of great wealth and culture,
who went about saying
to their fellow Jews,

"Let us go and make a covenant
with the gentiles living around us.
For ever since the day
we withdrew from their midst
and kept exclusively to ourselves,
much sorrow has come upon us."

The people listened
and many were pleased,
for they loved the culture of the Greeks—
the poetry, theater, philosophy,
the athletic contests and games—

some even liked the statues,
the beautiful sculptures, graven images,
and they coveted them.

Many Jews resented
their own religious leaders
who insisted they withdraw
from the Greek culture
and hold exclusively to their own.

Some of these Jews were so bold
as to appear before the king
to ask if they could once again
adopt the ways of the Greeks,
customs they formerly enjoyed
and now so deeply missed.

Antiochus Epiphanes listened attentively.
"Ah! I see!" he said.
"You want a bit of Athens
in Jerusalem,
with all the privileges
of both Athens and Jerusalem.
What a splendid idea!"
So he approved, and eagerly
gave them permission—
the "privilege" of following
the practices of the Greeks.

The very first thing these Jews did
was to build a gymnasium
in Jerusalem
on the Temple Mount,

close to the Temple,
so they could pray
and then play
without any delay!

Many Jewish athletes
even went to surgeons,
asking them to recreate foreskins,
for they were embarrassed
to be recognized as Jews
when they appeared naked
during the games.

Some Jews even ceased
circumcising their baby boys,
thereby forsaking the sacred Covenant
and joining themselves
willingly to the gentiles.

Some men began to bring women
to the Temple Mount,
to revel and party there with the gentiles—
even inside the Temple!—
drinking wine, laughing and joking,
and laying with whores
or girlfriends or other men's wives—
gentile women, Jewish women,
any sort of woman would do!
And some even lay with men.
They squandered their money
and became slaves
to the ways of the Greeks.

Even some priests
stopped serving the altar
and neglected the sacrifices.
Instead they ran eagerly to the gymnasium,
where they particularly enjoyed
the game called "throwing the discus,"
forgetting the honors due
to the Creator and to their fathers,
preferring sports and the glory of Greece.

Some men even converted
and worshiped the gods of the Greeks,
above all, Olympian Zeus,
whom the Greeks called "Father."
Some paid homage
to his son, Dionysus,
the god of the vine,
who promised eternal life
to those who believed in him—
and horrible death
to those who did not.

These converts delighted so
in the ways of the gentiles
and wanted so much to be like them,
many became enemies
of their own people
and began to persecute them.
How zealously they took their conversion!

Antiochus Epiphanes Conquers Jerusalem

In the 143rd year
of the Kingdom of the Greeks,   [169 B.C.E.]
Antiochus Epiphanes
decided to destroy
the people of Israel.

The Jewish converts
had alerted him
that many Jews
were still faithful
to the religion of their fathers.
They told him, too,
that in spite of the many Jews
who had adopted
the ways of the Greeks—
and who were willing
to play games,
even on the Sabbath,
and to give up the Covenant—
most of the Jews were still unwilling
to believe in the gods of the Greeks
and to give up a belief
in the Holy One of Israel,
the Creator of all mankind.

Antiochus entered Jerusalem
with a great army
but took the city without a fight,
because the Jewish converts
had told the faithful Jews

that Antiochus
was coming in peace.
The people believed this
and opened wide the gates to greet him.

In triumph, Antiochus Epiphanes
marched up the Temple Mount
into the Temple courts
and, in his arrogance,
into the sanctuary.

He carried away the altar of gold,
the seven-branched lampstand,
and all the furnishings—
the gold vessels, the gold censers,
the table of the ceremonial bread,
the pitchers, the cups, the bowls,
the curtains, and the crowns.

All the gold ornaments
decorating the Temple facade
he stripped off, pulled down,
and carried away.

Antiochus Epiphanes kept for himself
some of the choicest vessels,
and all the hidden treasure
he could find.

After he had taken these things,
he slaughtered the Jews
on the Temple Mount.

Then Antiochus Epiphanes
began his march home to Syria,
proceeding in triumph and splendor,
boasting proudly as he went
of all the wonderful things
that he had done
in Judea.

Israel's Lament

Great was the lamentation
throughout all Israel.
The leaders and old people
went into mourning,
and the young people mourned, too.
Men sobbed and wept like women,
and women wept incessantly.

Bridegrooms,
instead of making love
on wedding beds,
lay there lamenting,
and their brides grieved
at their sides.

The very land itself
went into mourning,
and no one
in all the House of Jacob
could be consoled.

Jerusalem Becomes a Greek City-State

For two whole years
the Jews mourned
the desecration of the Temple.

At the end of that time,
Antiochus Epiphanes
sent his chief magistrate
into all the cities of Judea
and ordered the Jews
to go to Jerusalem.
"This is very strange,"
the Jews said to one another,
for it was not the season
of a pilgrim festival.

All of Israel
went to Jerusalem,
entire families, with their servants.
And after they had assembled there,
the king's messenger spoke to them
of peace—
but in his heart
was treachery.

So convincing was he
that the people believed him
and began to rejoice.
While they were singing and dancing,
Antiochus Epiphanes attacked
with a mighty army
and smote Jerusalem.

BALLAD 1: ANTIOCHUS EPIPHANES

In the 145th year
of the Kingdom of the Greeks,   [167 B.C.E.]
Antiochus Epiphanes,
who had plundered the Temple
two years before,
now plundered Jerusalem.
He piled high the spoils,
tore down the houses,
and set them on fire.
He massacred many men
and took the rest,
along with the women and children,
as slaves.

Then
Antiochus Epiphanes
repaired the ancient City of David
and built a great wall with mighty towers.
He built there a Citadel for his soldiers,
gentiles and converted Jews—
those who liked to inflict harm
on the faithful children of Israel.
He equipped the Citadel
with weapons, stores of food,
and everything his men would need
to snare anyone
who went to the Temple.
What an evil adversary
against the people of Israel!

Whenever Jews
climbed to the Temple Mount,
soldiers in the Citadel killed them.

Innocent blood flowed
everywhere on the Mount
and down the mountainsides,
and the guards of the Citadel
polluted the Temple.

The inhabitants of Jerusalem fled,
and the city became unrecognizable—
a Greek city-state
foreign to her own children,
the children who deserted her.

"O Jerusalem!
Your Temple is desolate
like a wilderness.
Your joyous festivals are turned
into funeral rites,
glad songs into dirges,
happy Sabbaths into days of shame,
honor into contempt.

"Your glory is nowhere to be found.
Disgrace has taken its place.
Everything once exalted
is trampled in the dust,
and mourning is everywhere.
All majesty is vanished
from the daughter of Zion."

In the words of the prophet,
"A day of wrath is that day,
a day of distress and anguish,
a day of ruin and devastation,
a day of darkness and gloom,
a day of clouds and thick darkness."

Forced Conversion

Meanwhile, Antiochus Epiphanes
sent decrees everywhere in Syria
and its outlying provinces—
to his whole kingdom.

The king ordered
everyone to be one people
and to worship in one way,
the true way,
his way,
the way of the Greeks.
The Jews were to forsake the Torah,
their precious gift from the Creator.

Many Jews readily converted,
and almost all the gentiles did—
some willingly,
others through fear of being executed
if they did not comply.

53

And they worshiped Zeus,
Father most powerful,
and some also worshiped Dionysus,
son of Zeus, son of God.

They prayed before idols
and sacrificed to them.
They ate swine,
and they broke the Sabbath.

The king sent messengers
to Jerusalem and to all the towns
and cities throughout Judea, proclaiming:

"The Jews must follow
the laws of the Greeks,
for they are the laws of the land.
Hebrew laws are abolished.

"Jews must cease celebrating
the Sabbath and all their holidays.
They must treat them all
like ordinary days.

"The Temple priests
are to set up altars
with images
in sacred groves
and in the marketplace,
and they are to set up shrines with images.

"They are to sacrifice pigs
upon the altar

54

and eat them,
for nothing so delicious
can be 'unclean.'

"No male child shall be circumcised.
The human body is beautiful
and must not be mutilated."

By the king's decree,
the children of Israel
were forced to pollute their souls.

And the king was so bold
as to give these reasons:

"I am doing these things
in Israel's best interest,
that she may no longer be blind,
that she may see the truth,
that she may forget
the superstitious customs
and laws of her ancestors.
There no longer shall be
Jew and Greek
but all shall be one,
united in the universal religion
that includes everyone!

"Whoever refuses to obey
the decree of the king,
that person shall die."

Antiochus Epiphanes
sent the same message
to all the cities of Judea,
and he appointed supervisors
to see that the Jews obeyed.

The "Abomination of Desolation"

Jews wishing to be faithful
to the teachings of their fathers
had little choice.
If they stood their ground,
defied adoption of the "universal"
and "true" religion,
they faced certain torment,
torture, and death.
If they wanted to live,
they had to flee and go into hiding.

The "abomination of desolation,"
the detested ruination
of the stone altar of burnt offerings
in the Temple,
took place on the fifteenth day
of the month of Kislev,
in the 145th year
of the Kingdom of the Greeks.   [167 B.C.E.]
The altar was converted
into an altar to Zeus,
an altar for sacrificing swine.
Similar altars were set up

in every town and city
in Judea.

Jewish converts committed
countless acts of evil.
They were dangerous men.

Within the Temple
they set up a great idol to Zeus,
renaming that holy place
the "Temple of Olympian Zeus."
And they placed graven images
throughout all the towns
and cities of Judea,
and began to burn incense
to the statues,
just like the gentiles.

Wherever they found Torah scrolls,
they tore them to bits, set them on fire,
and burned them to ashes.

Whenever they discovered a man
studying Torah,
they tortured him
and put him to death.

Once a month
the inspectors made rounds
of the cities and towns,
as the king had ordered them to do,
to discover who

among the children of Israel
were studying their sacred teaching.

The twenty-fifth of every month
was set aside as a special day
for the Jews to sacrifice a pig
on the altar in the Temple
and on altars throughout the land.
After the sacrifice,
the pigs were roasted
and the people were forced to eat
the forbidden meat.

But many in Israel were resolved
not to eat the flesh of pigs.
They vowed they'd rather die—
and some of them did.

Eleazar
and the Mother and Her Seven Sons

When Antiochus Epiphanes
learned of the Jews
defying his decree,
he decided
he would have Jews
eat the flesh of pigs
before his very eyes.

He announced,
"Any Jew who refuses to eat pork

will be tortured and killed."
These things he planned to do in public,
a spectacle for all to see.
So he chose the top
of one of Jerusalem's hills,
surrounded himself with
a retinue of armed troops,
and commanded the spear-bearers
to seize every Jew they could find
still remaining in the city
and bring them before him.

After a sizable number of Jews
had been rounded up,
the king discovered
a prominent man among them—
a priest advanced in years,
a lawyer well-known and liked
even by the king's men.
His name was Eleazar.

Antiochus Epiphanes
had Eleazar brought before him
and said to him,
"Old man,
I see my men know you
and like you.
My advice to you
is to taste the flesh of swine
and live,
unless you prefer to be tortured
and die.

I respect you and your age,
which tells me
you have gained some wisdom.
So how can you continue to hold
the superstitious religion
of your countrymen?

"Since nature has provided
this most delicious of meats,
how can you despise it?
Reason says, 'Enjoy whatever is pleasant,
and abhor it not.'
Nothing so good can be sinful.
Accept nature's bounty.
That is the truth, old man.
How can you reject the truth?

"But if you reject my advice,
you court your own punishment.
Wake up!
Shake that insane religion from you!
Accept the wisdom that befits your age!
Accept the truth!
I am merely trying to be kind
to an old man.

"Bear in mind, too,
that if there really is a god
who watches over you,
he will surely forgive
any transgressions
you are forced to commit
against your will."

Eleazar responded,
"O Antiochus,
we believe we live under a divine law.
Therefore, there is no force so great
as obedience to that law.
You, on the other hand,
ridicule our religion
as if it were foolish and irrational.
Well, I cannot follow your decree.

"If our religion is not divine,
as you apparently believe,
even then we have no right
to discard it like refuse.
For it teaches us to be temperate
in all things
and to control our passions.

"Our religion encourages us
to show fortitude
in the face of adversity,
and it teaches us justice and fairness
in all our dealings
with our fellow man.
It teaches us to love God,
who created us and blesses us
and gives us everything.

"Our Creator, who gives us laws,
surely knows our nature
and sympathizes with it.

Surely the Creator knows
what is good for us
and what is not.
But you claim to know
more than the Creator.

"And you laugh at us.
Well, I do not think it is funny
to ridicule our God
and the religion of our fathers.
So prepare your torture;
add fuel to the fires.
I shall not forsake the Torah,
which is my teacher,
nor abandon the self-control I love,
nor put to shame
the manner of our thinking—
no, not if you pluck out my eyes
and burn my entrails.

"I have lived a full and good life,
and my fathers shall receive me pure,
not having submitted to force,
even unto death."

Thereupon
the spear-bearers took him
to the instruments of torture,
where they ripped off his clothing,
tied his arms behind his back,
and whipped him.

One of the king's friends
cried out in compassion,
"Obey the king, old man!"
But Eleazar only turned his eyes
to heaven.
The whipping continued,
ripping off the flesh
from his back and shoulders,
and making the blood flow.
Then the soldiers
pierced his sides with spears.

He fell down to the ground,
for his body no longer had the strength
to support itself.
One of the spearmen
lifted him up.

An attendant of the king
ran up to Eleazar and said,
"There is no need
to destroy yourself, Eleazar!
The king has told me
to bring you some lamb,
which you yourself have prepared.
Eat that! We will pretend it is pork,
and the king will let you go!"

The old Jew looked at him and said,
"This advice tortures me
more than the whip.
Let no child of Abraham

submit to such pretense!
I have lived my whole life through
in the service of truth.
How can I turn my back on it now?
What kind of example would I set
for the young,
who either would think I was eating pork
or would know I was practicing deceit?
I prefer to die than to live like that."

The soldiers escorted Eleazar to the fire.
And with their black instruments of death
heated to red,
they burnt him,
while pouring foul-smelling liquid
down his nostrils.
As he was dying he cried out,
"O God, be merciful to your people!
Let my blood redeem them
from their sins,
and let the loss of my life
by torture and death
save theirs."
Thus Eleazar died.

No sooner was he dead,
than Antiochus Epiphanes ordered
other Jews to step forth
and eat pork, saying,
"If you do so, I will let you go.
But if you refuse, I will torture you
worse than I tortured the old man."

BALLAD 1: ANTIOCHUS EPIPHANES

Seven brothers
were brought before the king,
along with their mother.
These young men
were handsome, well-mannered,
of noble bearing, and full of manly grace.

When the king saw them
all standing in a circle
around their mother—
as gracefully as if
they were dancing around her—
he was struck
by their surpassing good looks
and sincere demeanor.

He smiled at them
and told them to come near, saying,
"O youths,
I admire the beauty of each of you
and am filled with fond feelings
for every one of you.
I yearn to heap honors
on so many brothers.

"I advise you
not to share the madness of the old man
who has just been tortured,
but beg you to give in to my decree
and enjoy my friendship.
For I possess the power
not only to punish

those who disobey,
but to reward
those who are obedient.

"Trust in me, then,
and you shall receive
positions of authority
in my government,
if you only forsake your nation's ways
and conform to the Greek way of life.
Break your rules,
and revel in the delights of youth!

"If you provoke me by disobedience,
you will force me
to destroy every one of you
with terrible torture.
Have mercy, therefore, upon yourselves,
for although you are my enemy,
I am moved by your youth and beauty."

He then ordered
the instruments of torture
to be brought forth.
After the spearmen
had brought the wheels and racks,
the hooks and catapults,
the cauldrons and huge pans,
the iron hands and wedges,
the king continued:

"O youths, I advise you
to fear and obey me,

for the Righteousness you worship
will be merciful to you
if you are forced to sin."

The youths could have accepted
the king's argument,
but they did not.
On behalf of them all,
the eldest boy said,
"O tyrant king,
we prefer death to transgressing
the teachings of our fathers.
But do not pity us.
We suspect your pity
means a fate worse than death.

"Do you think
Eleazar's death has frightened us?
If you end up murdering us
because we are Jews,
how can you harm us by torture?
We shall inherit by our virtue
the rewards of eternal life.
On the other hand,
you, by your wanton and evil murders,
shall bring on yourself the wrath of God,
and you shall endure
eternal torture by fire."

The king was exasperated
and enraged.
He considered them ungrateful.

So he ordered the eldest to be first.
The spear-bearers tore the tunic
from his body
and bound his hands and arms.
After they had whipped him—
without effect—
a spearman said,
"Here is some pork. Eat it,
and you will be released."
The young man responded,
"Do what you will!
I shall show you
that the children of Israel,
alone of all the people on the earth,
remain unconquered
in the service of Righteousness."

The soldiers hurled him onto the wheel,
turned it,
and dislocated his joints,
all the while heaping new fuel
upon the fire.
The wheel was defiled
with the young man's blood and gore.
Some dripped upon the hot ashes
and sizzled,
while flesh was scattered
about the axles of the machine.

The youth did not cry out, but said,
"O Brothers! Courage!
Do as I have done.
Fight the good fight

of honor and holiness.
Heaven will punish this fiend."
Saying this, he died.

Then the spearmen
brought forth the second oldest
and bound him to the catapult
with iron hooks
anchored to the platform.
The king asked if he preferred torture
to eating pork.
"Yes," he said,
whereupon a spearman
wielding iron hands
clawed off the flesh
from his neck to his chin
and tore away all the skin
from his face and scalp,
as if he had been attacked
and mauled by a panther.

Without his face, he said,
"Think not, O King,
cruelest of tyrants,
that you will not suffer tortures
greater than mine.
My suffering is lightened
by the thought of the pleasures
linked with Righteousness.
For the Ruler of the Universe
shall raise us up into everlasting life.
My brothers and I die

as brothers in Torah!
But you, O King, shall not escape
the justice of God."

They slit his throat
and sprung the catapult.
His head flew into the air,
while his torso and limbs,
tied and anchored by hooks
to the platform,
remained behind.

The third brother was brought forth
and exhorted to taste pork
and save his life.
He said, "O King,
surely you must know
that my father
was the father of the dead men,
my brothers whom you murdered,
and we have the same mother,
and I was brought up
in the same house
and by the same teachings.
Apply your torture to my body;
you cannot touch
my invincible soul."

The racking engine
dislocated his hands and feet
and wrenched them
from their sockets,
and then proceeded

70

to dismember him.
The spearmen
dragged before the people
his hands and fingers,
his arms and legs,
his feet and ankles.
And still they whipped his torso,
tearing off the skin,
and placed him on the wheel,
which separated all his vertebrae.
He was able to see
his own flesh torn to shreds
and his own blood flowing in streams.
Just before he died, he said,
"We suffer for the sake of
our teachings of righteousness,
for our acts of kindness and generosity.
What will you suffer for your evil—
for your torment, torture, and murder?"

Then the spearmen
dragged the fourth brother
before the king.
A spearman said,
"Do not share the madness
of your brothers,
but respect the king
and eat some pork
and save yourself."

The boy replied, "There is no fire so hot
that it can conquer me.

71

By the blessed death
of my brothers
and by the glorious life
of the righteous
and by the eternal punishment
reserved for the king,
whatever new torture
you may devise and inflict on me,
I am the brother of those noble men
you tortured and murdered before."

Antiochus Epiphanes shouted,
"Cut out his tongue!"

The youth said, "Do you think
that God does not hear
those who are silent?
Cutting out the tongue
does not extirpate the mind.
It is good
on being put to death by men
to hold onto the hope
that comes from God
to be raised up again,
but you have no hope of that."
The boy's tongue was cut out,
and he was further mutilated
as he was tortured to death.

When he died,
the fifth brother jumped forward
and said, "O King,
I come before you of my own accord,

you hater of virtue and of mankind.
What have the Jews done to you
that you take such pleasure
in shedding our blood?
Do you consider us evil just because
we worship the Creator of all things
and live according to his teachings?

"What we do is worthy of honor,
not torture.
You would know this
if you were capable
of any human feelings
and if you possessed
any hope of salvation from God.
But you are far from God
and foreign to God,
to make war on those who love him."

The spear-bearers bound the youth
to the catapult,
fastening him with iron fetters.
They placed his loins
on the wedge of the wheel,
and his body was dismembered
so it looked like a scorpion's.
The youth said,
"O tyrant, what have we done
that you bestow such honors upon us
and make us suffer so nobly?"
At this they slit his throat
and sprung the catapult,

and his head
went flying into the air.

The sixth brother was brought forth.
The king asked if he would eat pork
and be saved.
The boy said, "Is eating pork
the gentile way to salvation?

"Dear Brother,
remember the stock
from whom you came,
and Abraham, Isaac, and Jacob
will receive us in heaven."

The spear-bearers took him to the wheel
and extended his body upon it.
With limbs racked and disjointed,
he was gradually roasted
on the fire beneath.
And they pierced his body
with sharp and red-burning spits—
some sticking into his back,
others transfixing his sides
and burning his entrails.

All the while he said,
"We have been called
to this contest of pain
and we have not been conquered!
Our religion has not been vanquished,
O deviser of torment
and enemy of righteousness!

You ordered us to defile our religion,
but we have not done so.
You have not conquered us!
We have conquered you!"
Then the youth was thrown
into the boiling cauldron.

At that the seventh and last brother,
the youngest of all,
came forth.
The king, seeing him in chains,
had him brought near.
Filled with pity,
moved by the boy's youth and beauty,
and feeling a gnawing discomfort,
the king said,
"You saw how all your brothers died,
needlessly, out of madness.
You will share the same fate
if you embrace disobedience.
But if you obey,
you shall be my friend,
and I shall place you in charge
of major affairs of the kingdom."

The boy was silent,
so the king sent for the mother,
all the while thinking
that having seen
all but one of her sons killed,
she might relent
where the last and youngest

was concerned,
and encourage him to save himself.

The mother went up to her son
and said something to him in Hebrew,
whereupon the boy
turned to a spearman and said,
"Release me!
I want to speak to the king
and his friends."
These rejoiced greatly
at the statement of the youth,
and the king told the spearman
to let him go.

Instantly,
running up to the giant frying pans,
the youth said, "O evil tyrant!
Are you not ashamed,
having received your riches
and your kingdom from God,
to rack and slay his servants,
doers of righteousness?
Are you not ashamed
to be called a man
when you are more savage
than a beast
to inflict such pain upon men,
to torture them,
to cut out their tongues,
to dismember them,
to decapitate them,
and only then to kill them?

"I who am about to die
will never forsake the things
my brothers have said and done.
And I call upon the God
of my ancestors
to be merciful to my people.
No doubt we suffer because of our sins,
yet we shall be forgiven
and become once again
the worthy servants of God.

"As for you and yours,
both living and dead,
and all others who have been
the authors of all manner of evil
against the Jews,
the Almighty who sees all things
will surely punish you
with eternal fire and torment!
But I, like my brothers before me,
sacrifice myself
for the sins of our nation."
Thereupon the boy hurled himself
into a hot pan and was fried.

All seven brothers,
as though running the race to immortality,
hastened on to death through torture.

As for the mother,
she chose the Hebrew religion

that leads to eternal life
over the conditional promise of a tyrant
concerning the safety of her sons.
She told each son,
"Although I carried you in my womb,
it was not I who gave you breath and life,
nor was it I who shaped
your marvelous body and limbs.
But I have no doubt
that the Creator who made you
and all the generations of men
and all things from the beginning out of nothing
will know how to create you again
and give you breath and life once more."

Still, she was tormented unto death
each time she witnessed one of her sons
undergoing torture and fire.
And when the moment came
when she herself was about to be seized,
the spearmen had no time to touch her,
for she threw herself onto the pile of corpses
turning to ash in the fire.

Antiochus Epiphanes,
at last thinking
he'd done enough evil for one day,
released the remaining Jews,
warning them that the same fate awaited them
if they persisted in the error of their ways.

Some of the Jews,
witnessing the horrible deaths,

said the martyrs achieved immortality
and eternal life;
that the land of the Jews was purified
because of them;
that they took away the sins of the nation;
that by the blood of such righteous ones
and their redeeming death
God saved Israel, until then afflicted
because of her sins.
And these people sang,
"Glory be to God forever and ever. Amen."

Ah! The power of the wishful thinking
of overpowered men!
They could not see
that the death of these martyrs
was murder, not sacrifice;
the Torah prohibits murder.
These deaths
were the outrageous and vengeful punishment
of an evil man,
not the sincere offerings
of a holy priest.
Moreover,
the Jews did not practice human sacrifice;
the Torah teaches its prohibition once and for all
that instant when God prevented Abraham
from sacrificing his son.
And so, one man's blood
cannot redeem another man's sins.
Even in cases of animal sacrifice,
the Torah teaches

the offering must be unblemished;
if a victim has so much as a bruise
prior to its slaughter—
let alone is tortured, mutilated, and bloodied—
it is no longer fit for holy sacrifice.

As for Antiochus Epiphanes,
he was amazed and filled with awe
at the unheard-of behavior and words
of the martyrs he had murdered
so ruthlessly that day.
He turned to his soldiers
and friends and said,
"In all things requiring nobility,
bravery, sincerity,
and endurance of suffering,
follow their example!"

Breaking the Covenant by Force

In addition to those
resolved not to eat pork,
many in Israel were resolved
not to break the sacred Covenant.

Whenever inspectors in Jerusalem
discovered a circumcised baby boy
at its mother's breast,
they raped the mother,
paraded her and the baby
throughout the city

to the top of the walls,
and then hurled mother and baby
headlong down.

Or else they plucked the baby
from the breast,
took the struggling mother,
and plunged a sword through her.
Then they placed a rope
around the baby's neck
and hung it from its mother's neck.

Sometimes they simply took the baby
and smashed its head against a wall,
dashing out its brains.

They searched all around for the man
who had performed the circumcision.
And if they found him,
they killed him, too.

Whenever people were found
secretly observing the Sabbath,
they were tied together
to a post on a pile of wood,
and the pile was set afire.
Israel suffered greatly.

As the prophet said,
"And the hills did tremble,
and their corpses were as refuse
in the midst of the streets."

Dogs ran through the city
and carrion birds were feasting.

Was all life to be
a countless succession
of intruders and invaders into Judea,
this tiny land?
Was all life to be
an endless succession
of murders of the Jewish people,
God's suffering servant?
Before the old wound
has time to heal,
a new wound
is inflicted upon the land
and upon the people.

"Out of the depths
I cry unto you, O YHV."*

"You feed your people
with the bread of tears
and give them tears to drink
in great measure."

"How long, dear God,
how long?"

YHV is a transliterated symbol of the ineffable name of God. Instead
of speaking it aloud, I suggest saying *God* or *the Creator* or *HaShem*.
See the introduction for a fuller explanation.

BALLAD 2
PTOLEMY PHILOPATOR

A Man Named Mattathias

In those days   [167 B.C.E.]
there lived a man named Mattathias,
the son of John,
who was the son of Simon,
a priest descended
from the family of Joarib,
which came from the town of Modin.

When Mattathias heard and saw
what Antiochus Epiphanes was doing,
he remembered the stories
he had heard as a child,
when his father and his grandfather
and his uncles and their friends
would talk about what was happening
to the Jews in Egypt
and other lands of the Diaspora.
Mattathias remembered especially
the suffering the Jews had endured
at the hands of Ptolemy Philopator.

*   *   *   *   *

Ptolemy Philopator Visits Jerusalem

Around the 95th year
of the Kingdom of the Greeks,   [ca. 217 B.C.E.]
Ptolemy Philopator was king of Egypt.
He was eager to visit Jerusalem
and its famous Temple,
for he had recently conquered Judea
and—for the time being—
taken it from Syria.

On his arrival in Jerusalem,
the king went immediately
to the Temple, to make sacrifices
and give thanksgiving offerings,
and do everything proper
to show his reverence
for that sacred place.

When he climbed the steps
to the inner court,
he was instantly struck
by the magnificence
of the building and the setting,
and he marveled at the beauty
of the architecture.
After gazing about in astonishment,
he announced his wish
to enter the sanctuary
and visit the holy of holies.

The priests respectfully told the king
that to enter the holy of holies

84

was forbidden
even to Jews, even to priests.
Only the high priest
could enter that holy place,
and only at a designated time
on a designated day
once a year.

Ptolemy was determined
and would not accept "no"
for an answer.

Thereupon a priest took down
a Torah scroll,
and read and translated the portion
that said these things
in the very words of the Creator.

After listening politely,
Ptolemy persisted, insisting
that an exception should be made
in his case,
for he was after all
the king of Egypt.
"Even though all but the high priest
are deprived of this honor,
I should be granted this privilege
because whenever I wish to enter
a temple of the heathens,
none of their priests ever forbids me
from doing so."

The priests replied,
"Perhaps the king had no right
to enter the temples of the heathens,
but the priests were too polite
to tell him so.
But even if the king had the right
in the temples of the heathens,
no one has that right here—
not this day."

"Well, since I did in fact
enter other temples,
whether rightly or wrongly,
should I not enter yours
with or without your consent?"

"With all due respect, my lord,
it is not we who do not give consent.
The decision comes
from Heaven itself."

The king was not swayed,
so great was his determination.
The countenance
of the priests changed,
turning as white as snow,
showing great anguish of soul
as fear indescribable
came upon them
and pain unbearable
seized their hearts.
Some of the priests fell down
and prayed to Heaven

that the king
would change his mind.

Others beseeched him
to listen to reason
and his own good judgment.
But the more the Jews implored,
the more adamant the king became.

At last,
even his own bodyguards
and his highest-ranking officers
tried to offer help in the crisis.
They tried to explain to the king
that this was no affront,
no insult to him,
that it applied equally
to all the kings of the earth,
and he must not take offense.
For it was the Creator himself
who made the decree
that absolutely no one—
no one!—
was allowed within.
But all their persuasion
was in vain.

By now the people of Jerusalem,
having learned what was taking place
within the Temple court,
came pouring out of their homes,
not only men, but women, too—

not a customary thing
for women to do.

The people crowded the streets
and ran up the Temple Mount
to the Temple gates,
creating a great uproar.

As the mob grew,
the swelling commotion
made an indescribable noise,
such that the very walls and grounds
of the sacred site
seemed to tremble
and contribute to the sound,
as if the Temple itself were crying out
that it preferred falling down
and crumbling
to becoming polluted and defiled.

Still the king was not deterred.
Slowly he began to walk
toward the great Temple door
when the noise reached a thundering
and terrifying roar.

Suddenly the king began to shake
like a reed in the wind.
Then he fell down
onto the pavement.

His bodyguards and officers,
witnessing the fainting of the king,

were struck with terror,
for they feared that he might die.
They immediately lifted him up
and carried him to the outer court,
where he quickly revived.

The king stood up,
trembling and flushed.
He brushed himself off;
then, pointing
to all the Jews before him,
threatened, "You shall pay for this!"

Then he departed in a rage,
and returned to his throne in Alexandria,
where his anger did not diminish
but only festered and grew.

Alexandria

At that time
Alexandria was a great
and cosmopolitan city,
teeming and bustling with people
from all parts of the world.
It had a large Jewish community,
and the Jews worshiped
in a temple there.

The king hitherto
had felt nothing but admiration
for the Jews.
Their contributions to the city
and to the nation's welfare
far outweighed
the contributions of others,
vastly exceeding
their small numbers.
The king had appreciated
their loyalty to him
and lived peaceably with them.
But now he completely changed.

Because of the perceived insult
from the Jews of Jerusalem,
Ptolemy decided to punish
the Jews of Alexandria.

So he had the following sign posted
outside the Jewish temple in Alexandria:

"No Jew may enter
without first making sacrifice
to the gods of this land.
Furthermore, all Jews must register.
Any Jew who resists
will be seized and put to death.
Moreover, all Jews from this day forth
are to wear on their clothing
an ivy leaf,
the symbol of Dionysus,
son of Zeus, son of God.

This will identify the Jews,
because their civil rights
are henceforth restricted."

To this, the king added
the following postscript:

"On the other hand,
any Jew who converts and is initiated
into the secret rites
of the mystery religion
devoted to the god Dionysus,
that Jew shall be exempt
and shall have equal rights
with all other citizens of Alexandria."

The mystery rites of Dionysus,
the god of the vine,
appealed to some of the Jews.
For Dionysus promised
eternal life to believers in him
and a horrible death to nonbelievers.

The sacred rites
in celebration of Dionysus
included the drinking of wine,
for the fruit of the vine
was the god's own fruit
and sacred to him,
and celebrants believed
that by drinking wine
they became united with the god.

Many worshipers drank so much
they became drunk and frenzied.
They tore off their clothing,
and, in their wild excitement,
engaged in copulation
of every imaginable sort.

This was highly appealing
to many of the gentiles
and some of the Jews, too.
But most of the Jews
were kept away
by restraint or inhibition
or love of their ancient religion.

Some of the Jews who served
in the king's court
submitted without hesitation
to the king's decree.
They thought thereby
they would receive promotions.

Others thought
that by bribing the king's officers
they would live unmolested.

The Jews who converted
immediately slandered the faithful Jews,
as converts are wont to do,
calling them enemies
of the Egyptian people,
enemies of mankind,
and friends only to each other.

On hearing the slander,
the king believed it
and became so incensed
that he no longer confined his rage
to the Jews of Alexandria
but extended it to include
the Jews everywhere in Egypt.

He gave orders that all the Jews
be rounded up into one place
as quickly as possible,
and there most cruelly murdered.

Rumors

While this was going on,
an invidious rumor
began to circulate—
that the Jews broke the laws of Egypt
and encouraged others
to break them, too.

The Jews in fact
did not do certain things
that other people did.
They did not work on the seventh day
nor eat the flesh of pigs.
Although these customs did not conflict
with Egyptian law,

they set the Jews apart,
making them appear exclusive.
That alone
made many people hate them.

Their enemies,
out of envy and spite and malice,
said that the Jews were hostile
to the king's interests.
Such lies
brought widespread hatred upon them.

Living in Egypt at this time
was a community of Greeks
who had come from Athens and Sparta.
The uproar against the Jews
took these people by surprise,
and most of them refused to spread
the rumors that were flying.

Communities of Jews and Greeks
had lived together in amity
for many generations.
So the Greeks now
wanted to help their friends
and neighbors.
But it was not in their power
to do so,
the oppression was so widespread.

Still,
they gave the Jews encouragement,
expressing sympathy,

saying they fully expected
the situation to soon improve:
"The God of the Jews
will surely not forget
so great a people."

Some Greeks—neighbors, friends,
and business associates of Jews—
called a secret meeting
and pledged to do
everything they could to help.

The King's Decree

Now Ptolemy, king of Egypt,
greatly taken with himself
and with no thought of the possibility
of the existence of a god
more powerful than himself,
continued to act
in this outlandish way.

He wrote the following letter
to his army:

> From King Ptolemy Philopator
> to his commanders and soldiers
> throughout Egypt:
> Health and happiness!

MACCABEE

I am well, as are my affairs.
Ever since our victorious Eastern campaign . . .
we have resolved . . .
to take good care of the inhabitants
of the conquered places
and be their willing benefactors.

Having bestowed
considerable sums of money
on the temples in the cities
of these places,
we proceeded as far as Jerusalem
and went up to honor the temple
of those miserable wretches
who never cease from their madness.

To outward appearances
they received us gladly;
but their deceit became apparent
by the things they did thereafter.

When we were eager
to enter their temple,
and to honor it
with exquisite gifts,
the Jews were so carried away
by their old arrogance
as to forbid us the right of entrance.
Out of our forbearance toward all men,
we refrained from exercising
our power over them.

In thus showing their enmity to us,
they alone
among all the nations of the earth
reveal themselves

BALLAD 2: PTOLEMY PHILOPATOR

as a disobedient people
unwilling to submit
to reasonable authority.
The Jews alone refuse to bow down
before kings and benefactors!

Trying to make allowances
for the madness of these people,
on our victorious return
we treated all the people in Egypt
with the love of humanity
that is only fitting.
Accordingly,
bearing no ill will
against their kinsmen in Jerusalem,
but rather remembering our connection
with the Egyptian Jews
and the numerous matters
entrusted to them
going way back in time,
we wished to try a total alteration
of their prior lowly state
by bestowing upon them
and giving them
the full rights of citizens of Alexandria,
including admission
to the rites of eternal life
afforded by our solemn religion
of mysteries.

However,
all this benevolence on our part
they took in a very different spirit.
With their innately hateful spirit,
they spurned my generous offer.

Constantly inclined to evil,
they rejected these invaluable rights.
By the things they said—
as well as by the things
they did not say—
they showed how much
they hated the few Jews among them
who were readily obedient to us,
ever believing
that their base course of action
somehow will force us to cease
from our measures to reform them.

Having then received proof
that the Jews bear us every sort of ill will,
we have no choice but to take action
against the possibility
that these evil men
will foment a revolution in our streets
when they eventually decide
to become traitors
and barbarous enemies.

Therefore,
as soon as you receive this letter,
we order you to send us immediately
the Jews who dwell among you,
along with their wives and children,
to be vilified and abused,
to be placed in chains of iron,
and to undergo a most cruel and base death
altogether befitting such a rebellious people.

For by punishing them as one body,
we think we have found
the only means

of placing affairs for the future
on a firm and satisfactory basis.

Therefore,
let it be known
that whoever shall hide or protect a Jew
shall with his whole family
and everyone in his household
be tortured to death.
By contrast, whoever informs on a Jew,
besides receiving the property
of the Jew so charged,
shall be rewarded abundantly
from the royal treasury,
will have guarantees of perpetual freedom,
and will receive other great honors besides.

Whatever place shall shelter a Jew,
that place on discovery shall be set on fire
and rendered uninhabitable
to every living being forever.

That was the king's decree.

Rounding Up the Jews

Wherever the decree was published,
many Egyptians shouted
and jumped and danced for joy.
Long envious of the Jews,
they could now display openly
their pent-up, adamant hatred.

The Jews suffered miserably
from pain and sorrow.
Their hearts were broken
by the king's decree,
not only by its content,
but by its swiftness
and destructiveness.

What home or city
or place inhabited by human beings,
what street or lane was not filled
with weeping and lamentation?

The commanders sent the decree
to all the cities of Egypt.
And it was delivered
with such harsh and pitiless feeling
that the extraordinary nature
of the infliction
upset even some of those
who hated Jews the most.

They were moved by feelings
of common humanity
and the universal plight
of the human condition.
They understood
that whatever could happen
to the Jews
might one day,
for one reason or another,
happen to them.

Reflecting on the uncertainties of life,
a few of these people even shed a tear
at the miserable treatment and expulsion
of their former friends and neighbors.

Deportation

The king's soldiers
pushed and shoved many old people,
stooped over by age
and walking with faltering footsteps,
goading them on
with impulsive, violent, swift,
and shameless force.

Young brides enjoying marriage
exchanged that pleasure
for misery;
and with dirt
hurled at their bridal crowns
were hurried along
to the shouts of outlandish insults—
"Slut!" "Jewish whore!"
"Hey, there, my beauty,
give me a little kiss!"

Bound and exposed
to the public gaze and taunts,
they were hurried violently
on board the waiting boats.

Husbands in the prime of youth,
instead of wearing garlands of flowers,
wore halters around their necks;
instead of delighting
in the pleasures
of the marriage bed,
they spent the rest
of their honeymoon days
weeping and sobbing,
a vision of the grave
before them.

Like wild animals
they were dragged and yanked
by unyielding chains
on board the ferries and barges
lined up along the canal,
where they were thrust
into rowing benches,
their feet locked in fetters of iron.
The tight-fitting planks
of the deck above
and the absence of portholes below
barred daylight on every side.
And they were treated
like slaves or traitors
during the trip.

The Racetrack at Schedia

The boats docked at Schedia,
a suburb of Alexandria,
on the canal.
The king ordered the Jews
to be taken and thrown into cells
beneath the great racetrack
that stood outside the town.
There were enough seats at the track
for all who wished to come
and witness the spectacle.

The Jews were not allowed
to speak to their guards,
for Jews were deemed
unworthy of human intercourse.
All the Jews of Egypt
were to be locked up in cells
and registered.

Every person
was to be specified by name,
not for the purpose
of recording the names of slaves,
but for the sole purpose
of duly recording the name
of every Jew who died
on the day designated
for their annihilation.

The registration
was carried out
ruthlessly,
cruelly,
zealously,
assiduously,
from the rising of the sun
to its setting,
and the registration was not over
even after forty days.

The king was filled
with great and constant joy;
he celebrated
with sumptuous banquets
held before the idols in the temples.
He spoke
of the glory of graven images
and ridiculed
the god of the Jews.

On the day the registration
was supposed to have been completed,
the registrars complained to the king
that there were not enough of them
to do the great amount of work,
for there were simply too many Jews.
Many of those in the country
were not yet accounted for.

The king grew angry.
He accused the registrars
of hiding Jews

in the homes of complicit gentiles.
And he accused his officers
of taking bribes
to help the Jews escape.

The Extermination Plan

It was the king's intention,
once all the Jews were registered
and gathered together
at the great racetrack,
to have elephants released at daybreak
to trample the Jews to death.

The king sent for Hermon,
the trainer of the elephants.
After giving his orders,
which were to be carried out
the next morning,
he ordered Hermon
to feed the beasts—
there were five hundred of them—
great quantities of undiluted wine
mixed with plenty of incense
before turning them loose
on the Jews.

The king asked the royal cook
to prepare a breakfast banquet
to be held at the racetrack

for his friends and officers.
Then, while feasting on breakfast,
they could watch—
for their entertainment—
elephants trampling Jews to death.

That evening the children of Israel,
chained and fettered,
prayed to the merciful Creator.

Next morning before dawn,
they were brought onto the track,
security precautions having been taken
so that none should escape,
and all would perish together.

Then Hermon fed the elephants
great quantities of wine mixed with incense,
as the king had instructed him to do.

The king's guests were all assembled,
and the banquet table was spread.
But where was the king?

Hermon ran to the palace
to tell the king that things were ready,
exactly as he had ordered,
and that the only thing missing
and delaying the show
was the king himself.

Hermon went
into the king's bedroom
and found him there,
sound asleep and snoring.
He shook the king
but could not rouse him
except with difficulty,
whereupon he would fall
right back to sleep.

Finally, Hermon gained
the king's attention
and reminded him
about the banquet
that was already taking place
and the spectacular show
that could not begin
without his presence.

He helped the king to dress,
and they drove to the track
at full speed
in the royal chariot.

On the king's entry,
his guests arose and saluted him.
Now composed,
the king requested
that they resume their places
and enjoy themselves,
even though they had already
finished their breakfast.

Morning was rapidly ending,
and the day was already hot.

The king's guests
had feasted on juices,
fish and eggs, breads, cheeses,
honey, and fruits;
but the king would have none
of these.
He wanted only wine.

The conversation was lively
and focused on the Jews,
how they had not perished
but somehow
had managed to escape death.

The king, on hearing this,
turned to Hermon
and angrily asked,
"Why are the Jews still alive?"

Hermon explained that he had done
just as the king had commanded.
The king's friends confirmed
Hermon's report.
Slamming down his silver cup
and bending it out of shape,
the king flew into a rage,
shouting and sputtering
in somewhat slurred speech,

"Are you shaying
the Jews are shtill alive
because the king overshlept?
You fool! You blind fool!
Begin preparations immediately
so that firsht thing tomorrow
those accurshed Jews
will be deshtroyed!"
Then the king was driven
back to his palace.

The next morning
just after the cock crowed,
Hermon began feeding
the elephants the concoction
of wine and incense again.
Once more the king's friends
were enjoying
a breakfast banquet at the track,
while crowds from the city
were gathering
to watch the hideous spectacle.

All were waiting impatiently
for the dawn to appear
and the show to begin.
The Jews were led onto the track.
They lifted their arms to heaven
and prayed.

Hermon went to the palace.
This time the king was ready.
Hermon and the king
hastened to the track,
and the king took his seat
among his distinguished guests.
He lifted his cup of wine,
smiled broadly at his friends,
looked out upon the Jews,
and with a quizzical look
inquired,
"Why are there Jews out there?"

Hermon replied,
"The elephants are ready, my lord.
You have only to give the word,
and the great beasts will be released."

Again the king said,
"Why are there Jews out there?"

Then, scrutinizing Hermon's face,
the king said,
"You know, Hermon,
I could understand it
if your parents
or your wife and children
were out there,
waiting for execution
by those mighty
and magnificent beasts,
but why Jews?
They are innocent!

110

They have always
served me well—
and my ancestors, too.
It would make more sense
if *you* were out there—
not *Jews*!"

Hermon was puzzled.
He was also alarmed.
He was not expecting the king's threat,
and could not hide
the frightened expression on his face.
Anxious and embarrassed,
the king's friends slunk out
one by one—
and soon the announcers
sent the crowds home.

The elephants,
which were standing at the gates,
were taken back to their cages,
and the king
was taken back to the palace
and tucked into his bed.
The Jews were spared,
and lived to see another day.
They abundantly praised the Creator
and gave him thanks.

The next day
the king did not rise until noon.
He told Hermon

that the following morning at dawn
he was planning to give
another banquet at the track.

Then he said to Hermon angrily,
"Hermon, you stupid man,
how often do I have to give you
the same order
about these same horrible people?
Pay attention
and do what I tell you to do!
Prepare the elephants
to go out tomorrow morning
and trample the Jews to death!"

The king's wife—
who was also his sister—
was present at the time,
as was his mistress
and her brother.

On hearing the king's comments,
they all wondered about his stability.
The queen said,
"My lord and my god,
this is the third time
you have ordered
the destruction of the Jews.
As soon as the thing
is about to be done,
you change your mind.
These changes have aroused
changing expectations

on the part of the people,
causing them great agitation."

The king responded angrily,
"You speak to your husband and god like this?
You worthless piece of camel dung!
When have I ever changed my mind?
Tomorrow the Jews shall be annihilated
by the great beasts!
That has always been my intention!
And after that, I will invade Judea
and level its towns with fire and sword.
I will destroy the Temple—
which *NO GENTILE MAY ENTER*—
and prevent sacrifices
from ever again
being offered there!"

Death by Elephant

The next morning
the elephants were given
more wine and incense than ever before,
which drove them into a frenzy.
Every seat at the racetrack was filled.
The king entered,
and with pitiless eyes
stared out at the Jews,
for he was looking forward
to their hideous doom.

113

The Jews, on seeing
the elephants staggering onto the track
from the gates
and the soldiers of the king
following the animals,
and on seeing the dust
raised up in clouds
by the tottering elephants
and the marching soldiers,
and on hearing the stamping
and shouting of the crowd,
were certain they had come
to their end.

Through their weeping
they uttered such a loud cry
to heaven
that the hills and valleys resounded,
calling forth
from some of the king's troops
irrepressible tears and sobs
and choking.

The Jews
began to kiss one another good-bye.
Fathers and mothers embraced
sons and daughters;
babies clung to mothers' necks,
and children clutched at their parents.
Husbands clung to wives
and wives to husbands.

114

The elephants
were released from the chains
attached to the harnesses
on their great bodies.
And then a remarkable thing occurred.

The beasts went berserk
and suddenly turned on their trainers
and on the king's army,
and proceeded to trample them to death—
every one!
But the Jews
they completely ignored!

The crowd was horrified.
A cold shudder came over the king.
He fell suddenly to the ground
and was surrounded in thick darkness,
just like that day in Jerusalem
when he wanted to enter the Temple.

When he revived,
his wrath had vanished.
He was smiling,
and his face was beaming
and emanating the purest light!
He had never known
such peace and happiness.

He gazed out upon the track
and was filled with awe
and compassion

when he saw all his men lying dead,
the elephants standing over them,
hardly moving;
and he heard the soft weeping
of the Jews, and saw them
standing in bewilderment,
only a moment before
on the brink of destruction,
and now completely unharmed.

The king, tears streaming
down his cheeks,
turned to face his party—
officers, governors, and friends—
and said,

"You have managed things badly,
exceeding all tyrants in cruelty.
And you have tried to deprive me,
your king and benefactor,
of my kingdom and my life
by secretly devising measures
harmful to the kingdom
and its finest treasures.
You have gathered here,
totally without reason,
removing from their homes,
these people who have shown
only loyalty to us
and have always been the strength
and bulwark of our nation,
even though their numbers are so few.

"Who has done this?
Who has assigned
this undeserved punishment
to those who have shown
nothing but goodwill toward us
from the beginning,
and have in all things and all ways
surpassed all peoples and all nations,
and who so often
have shown great courage
by engaging in the most dangerous
of enterprises and undertakings?

"Loose the unjust bonds!
Set the Jews free!
Send them back to their homes!
Shame on you for what you've done!
Shame! For shame!

"Release the sons of God,
the sons of the living Creator,
the Almighty God,
who, from the time of our ancestors
until this very moment,
has granted such glorious
and uninterrupted prosperity
to the Egyptian nation,
its people, and its affairs."

Celebration

So the king released the Jews,
who praised the Creator,
their Savior.

The king then called his financier
and told him to provide a feast
for the Jews, in their honor,
with the finest food—
and, of course, plenty of wine.
And he decided that the festival
should take place on the racetrack,
the very place
where the Jews had expected
to meet their total destruction.

So those
who only a moment before
had been despised
and on the brink of death
were now reprieved and exalted.
And the racetrack
intended for their fall and burial
was transformed
into a place of banqueting
and great celebration
and cheer.

The King's Letter

The king then wrote a letter
to his generals throughout Egypt,
and to all his governors, saying:

> From King Ptolemy Philopator
> to the commanders
> everywhere in Egypt
> and to all who govern:
> Joy and Strength!
> We are well,
> and our children are well, too!
>
> Almighty God has directed
> and accomplished our affairs
> exactly as we wished!
>
> It has come to our attention
> that certain of our friends,
> out of sheer malice,
> have most vehemently urged us
> to punish
> the Jews of our kingdom
> as a body
> with the infliction
> of a monstrous punishment.
>
> These wicked men pretended
> that Egyptian affairs
> could never run smoothly
> with Jews around,

119

for the Jews, they said,
were a people
who hated all peoples
but themselves.

So these friends of ours
chained and fettered the Jews
like slaves or traitors.
Without inquiry or trial,
they meant to annihilate them,
to carry out savage cruelty
worse than the barbarian nations.

Because we followed their advice,
we severely threatened the Jews.
Fortunately
our innate benevolence
to all men
made us come to our senses,
and we permitted the Jews to live.
We also discovered
that God in heaven
protects them, preserves them,
and fights for them,
as a father always fights
for his sons.

Taking into consideration
their constant fidelity
to our ancestors and to us,
we have, as is fitting,
acquitted them of every charge.
And we are sending them back

to their homes,
bidding all people everywhere
to do them no wrong
and not to slander them
any more.

Should anyone hatch—
or even conceive—
an evil plot against them,
or should anyone in any way
bother them,
he shall ever have as his enemy,
not man, but the highest God,
the Almighty Ruler of the Universe,
avenger of all evil.
From Him there can be no escape.
I have spoken.

The Trip Home

The Jews sang songs of thanksgiving
as they marched in joy
to the canal,
where the king's boats
were waiting
to carry them back
to Alexandria.

On returning home,
they received back

all their seized property;
and those who had stolen it
returned it with fear and trembling.

And the king, Ptolemy Philopator,
never again harmed the Jews,
but only showered them
with honors.

* * * * *

Mattathias never forgot this story.
He knew it could have had
a different ending.
Life in the Diaspora
was, in fact,
unpredictable.

BALLAD 3
MATTATHIAS

Mattathias and His Sons

When Mattathias was a young man,
before Antiochus Epiphanes
assumed the throne,
Mattathias had gone to Jerusalem
to find himself a wife.
A cousin introduced him
to a young girl,
fair to look upon,
named Irene Naomi.
Everyone called her Irene,
which means "peace"
in the Greek language.
Mattathias loved her,
and they were married
in the home of his cousin.

Mattathias built a home
for himself and his wife
in Jerusalem
and dwelled there.
And Irene bore five sons.

The first son was named John,
in memory of Mattathias's father.
At birth he was surnamed Gaddi
from the Persian word *gatza*,
meaning "royal treasure,"
for treasure he surely was—
a first-born child and a beautiful baby boy.

The second son was named Simon,
in memory of Mattathias's grandfather.
When Simon was a youngster,
he was surnamed Thassi
from the Greek word meaning "swifter,"
because Simon was swifter of foot—
and swifter of mind—
than the other children
living near and round about him.

Everyone admired Simon,
especially Mattathias.
On the day Simon was born,
Mattathias said of him
in the words of the prophet,
"For unto us a child is born,
unto us a son is given.
And the government
is upon his shoulder;
and his name is
Pele yo-etz el gibbor avi-ad sar-shalom,
which means
'A wonderful Counselor
is Almighty God, everlasting Father,
Prince of peace.'"

As Simon grew
into young manhood
he dropped the name Thassi,
for it embarrassed him
because it set him apart.
And he never adopted the name
Pele yo-etz el gibbor avi-ad sar-shalom.

Whenever a difficult problem
arose in the community,
Mattathias would turn to Simon,
who would readily come forth
with a solution.
Mattathias admired Simon
for his good judgment
and common sense,
and respected and loved him.

Next came Judah,
named in memory
of his mother's father, Judas.
Judah was the one,
as we shall see,
who would be called Maccabee.

Judah was of ruddy complexion,
and he had beautiful eyes.
He was handsome,
and his appearance and manner,
even as a child,
attracted people's attention.

Whenever Judah passed by,
young girls blushed and giggled,
young women smiled,
and men and women of all ages
engaged him in a pleasant word or two.
Occasionally someone would give him
a fig or a date or a sweet cake.

Everyone loved Judah—
everyone, that is, but bullies.
Judah loved to fight
other children's battles,
and he made them his own.
Whenever a bully attacked a small boy,
Judah was there to protect him
and fight for him.
There was no bully so big or so strong
that he was not afraid of Judah.

Judah's mother,
on washing his cuts and scratches,
would smile at him and say,
"My son, do you intend to fight
all the bullies of Israel?"
Then her eyes would fill with tears
as she said,
"Yes, I can see that one day
you will do even that!"
And she kissed him
on both of his beautiful eyes
and on both of his beautiful hands.

Next came Eleazar,
named in memory
of Irene's grandfather.
When Eleazar was a boy,
he was surnamed Avaran
from the Greek word meaning
"the shaft of a spear"
or the tree
from which the shaft is made,
for he was tall and strong,
limber and straight.

But a shaft,
however straight and strong,
limber and long,
needs a sharp point to be a spear.
And Avaran was dull.
Still, he was hardworking and earnest.
And once he started a task,
he saw it through to completion.

The youngest son was Jonathan,
named for Irene's own brother,
who had died in infancy.
He was surnamed Apphus
from the Greek word meaning "Papa,"
but his family called him Abba,
meaning "Papa" in Hebrew,
for as soon as he could smile,
he reminded his mother
of her own father.

Jonathan had a twinkle in his eye
and a delightful personality.
He was full of charm,
had a ready laugh,
and made others laugh, too.
He was fun to be around
for he made people feel good
about themselves—
just like Irene's papa did.
And his brothers loved Jonathan
best of all.

His father thought,
"Jonathan is bright
and brave enough,
but he is too eager to please
and a trifle too vain
and too trusting."
But Mattathias kept his thoughts
to himself.

One day
a neighbor huge with child
went into labor.
Irene was sent for to help the midwife,
for Irene could always be counted on
to help neighbors in distress.
She brought along
John Gaddi, her eldest son,
to play with the neighbor's children,
for John, like his mother,
enjoyed helping people in need.

128

After a long and hard labor,
the woman gave birth
to a beautiful baby girl.
Irene and John were returning home
at dusk, when Irene stumbled
and struck her head upon a rock,
losing consciousness.

John ran home shouting,
and Mattathias came at once.
He lifted his wife in his arms
and carried her home,
then sent for the surgeon,
who did everything he could,
but he could not save her.

The funeral was full of sorrow
beyond sorrow,
not only because
of the dead young mother,
who had been
a woman of understanding
and beauty,
but especially because
of the five motherless boys.

Family, friends, and neighbors
gathered round
to give comfort and consolation.

They said these words of Scripture:
"YHV gives and YHV takes away.
Blessed be the name of YHV."

They buried her,
and a neighbor sounded
the ram's horn trumpet,
"Ta RA, ta RA, ta RAA."

But the five sons of Irene
could not be comforted.
They could not be consoled.
They could not bless God's name.

They could not understand
why their mother
had been taken away
by the God who was so good.

After Irene's death,
Mattathias and his sons
continued to live in Jerusalem.
The boys became youths
and the youths became young men.

Then came that day   [169 B.C.E.]
when Antiochus Epiphanes
captured the city,
polluted the Temple,
and drove out the Jews.
Mattathias and his sons fled Jerusalem
and returned to Modin,
the town of their ancestors.

130

Mattathias's Lament

When Mattathias saw the sacrilege
committed in Jerusalem
and throughout Judea,
he cried out,

"Why was I born—
to witness this misery on my people,
this misery on Jerusalem?
To be living here at the moment
the city and the Temple
surrendered to gentiles?

"The Temple has been ravaged
and stripped of her glory,
her beautiful vessels
carried into captivity.

"The city's infants and children
have been slain in the streets,
her youth by the enemy's sword.
What nation has not stolen
a piece of Jerusalem
and claimed it as its own?

"What kingdom
has not plundered her?
All her adornments
have been carried away.
Once a free woman,
now she is a slave.

131

"Behold and see!
The Temple, once our glory,
the beauty of our country,
has been violated,
and the gentiles have polluted her.

"With all these sorrows heaped on us,
what is the purpose of living?"

Then Mattathias and his sons
rent their clothing,
put on sackcloth,
and grieved bitterly,
saying these words of David:

"O YHV our God,
to whom vengeance belongs,
shine forth!
Rise up!
Judge of the earth,
render to the arrogant
their recompense!
How long, YHV, how long
shall the wicked triumph?"

"Follow Me!"

While the house of Mattathias   [167 B.C.E.]
and all of Israel were grieving,
the king's officers,

enforcing the king's decree,
entered the town of Modin
to sacrifice to the gods and idols.

Many of the Jews,
among them Mattathias and his sons,
approached the officers
to speak to them.

A captain of the king
said to Mattathias,
"You are a leader in this town,
a great and distinguished man.
The people respect you,
and you have been blessed
with strong and brave sons.
So I call upon you first.

"Step forward,
and be the first in this town
to carry out the king's decree,
just as the gentiles have done—
and many men of Israel, too,
including those
who still remain in Jerusalem.

"It's not so hard to do.
After all,
your religion is antiquated
and superstitious—
a stumbling block
to the whole civilized world.

"Do as I say,
and you and your house
shall be counted
among the king's friends.
You shall be honored
by the king
with silver and gold
and other rewards in abundance.

"And remember,
if you are not with the king,
you are against him.
Are you with the king?"

Mattathias listened respectfully,
then responded in a loud voice,

"Though all the gentiles
from all the nations
under the dominion of the king
obey him out of fear
or desire to please him,
and though every one of them
is readily willing
to forsake the religion
of his ancestors,
even so, my sons and I
and the people of Israel
shall continue to walk
in the way of our religion.
We will never forsake
our love of the Creator,

the Ruler of the Universe,
and his commandments.

"We will pay no heed to you
or to the words of the king.

"Can anyone say
of the gods of the king,
'Where shall I go
from your holy spirit?
Where shall I flee
from your presence?
If I ascend to heaven,
you are there.
If I make my bed with the dead,
you are there.
If I take the wings of the morning
and dwell
in the uttermost parts of the sea,
even there
you take me by the hand
and lead me.'

"No one can say that of your gods.

"This is what one can say
of your gods,
'Your idols are stone, silver, or gold—
the work of men's hands.
They have mouths but do not speak,
eyes but do not see.
They have ears but do not hear,

and they do not utter a sound.
Those who make them are like them.
And so are all who trust in them.'

"You can believe in them
if you like.
That is your right
and that is your privilege.
But you cannot make us
believe in them.
You have no right to do that."

When Mattathias finished
speaking these words,
a Jew came forth
from the midst of the people.
And in sight of all,
he stepped up to the altar at Modin
to sacrifice a pig
in accordance with the king's decree.

Lifting his hands and eyes
to the image of Zeus before him,
the man said,
"O Zeus, our Father,
our Lord, and our Savior,
greatest of gods—
greater by far
than the god of the Jews—
I sacrifice this pig to you.
Grant long life
to our glorious king,
Antiochus Epiphanes,

who has shown us your glory
and opened our eyes
to the way of your truth!"

Then he raised his knife
and sacrificed the pig.
The blood squirted and flowed
over the altar and down its sides.

When Mattathias saw and heard this,
he was overcome with emotion.
Rage took possession of him
completely.
Every muscle in his body
strained and pulled
on all the tendons.
Hard as he tried,
he could not contain the anger
tugging and surging within him
with gigantic force.
No amount of reason
could hold him back.
He was like a volcano
in eruption.

Mattathias ran
and fell upon that man
and killed him on the altar.
Then he slew the officer
who was enforcing
the king's decree.
Then he knocked down the altar.

All these things he did
in the blink of an eye.

Then Mattathias shouted so loudly
the whole town of Modin
could hear,

"All who love Torah
and all who wish to keep the Covenant,
follow me!"

Then Mattathias and his sons
fled to the mountains,
leaving behind
all their possessions.

The resistance to tyranny
had begun.

BALLAD 4
IN THE WILDERNESS

The Sabbath Massacre

The Jews living in Modin
and all the towns
near Jerusalem
who still believed
in righteousness, justice,
and Heaven's judgment
fled into the wilderness
to dwell in caves and dens
like wild animals,
for conditions in the towns
were intolerable.

When the king's army
stationed in Jerusalem
learned of the Jews
who had defiantly disregarded
the king's decree
and had gone into hiding
in the wilderness,
the army pursued them
and caught up with some of them—
a thousand unarmed farmers and shepherds

from a village south of Modin—
just before sunset
at the start of the Sabbath.

The army pitched camp.
It was their intent
to attack the next morning.

At daybreak
an officer of the king's army
approached these Jews and said,
"Whatever you've done so far,
let this be the end of it
and we shall forget it all.
Just come forward
and give yourselves up.
Promise to obey
the king's ordinance
from this time forth,
and you shall live."

The Jews answered,
"We will not step forward
and give ourselves up,
nor will we
break the Sabbath."

"We will die, if die we must,
without any guilt-stain on us,
as innocent victims.
Heaven and earth
shall be our witnesses
that you wrongfully

put us to death.
And if you do that,
the Creator will raise us up
to everlasting life."

The army of gentiles
looked in amazement
at these people
on that Sabbath day.
Then the army rose up
and charged with all speed,
shouting battle cries,
and attacking them
as if they were a mighty force.

The Jews stood silent and still
because it was the Sabbath—
a holy day,
a day for reflection, refreshment, and rest.
They did not bend down
to pick up a single stone
to defend themselves,
nor try to hide.

The army slew them all—
men, women, and children
along with their livestock.

On that day,
one thousand innocent
men, women, and children—
not to mention many sheep and goats—

lost their lives
in a brutal massacre.

A Momentous Decision

When Mattathias
and his band from Modin
learned of this,
they mourned those people
from the village south of Modin.
They wept and filled the air
with cries of lamentation.
Finally Mattathias said,
"If we all do
as these poor people have done
and refuse to fight for our lives
on the Sabbath,
we shall soon be rooted
out of the earth.
And once we are gone,
who will celebrate
and rejoice in the Sabbath?"

All of them realized the truth
in what he said.
So this is what they decided:

"If we are attacked
on the Sabbath,
we will fight.
In that way at least

not all of us shall die
like our fellow Jews.
For Heaven clearly intended
that we should defend ourselves,
even on the Sabbath."

A group of Hasids—
religious men who opposed
everything Greek for Jews,
champions of the teachings
of their ancestors,
strong and brave men,
and decisive, too—
came to join them.
They agreed to suspend
the Sabbath rules
when self-defense was at stake.
Others came
fleeing persecution
and joined them,
and became part of the resistance.

Wherever they found
converted Jews who slandered
and tried to kill faithful Jews,
they slew as many as they could.
Those who escaped
ran over to the gentiles.

Jonathan and Rachel

While Mattathias and his sons
were in the wilderness
with other families from Modin,
Jonathan Apphus
noticed a comely young girl
named Hermione Rachel.
Her family called her Rachel.

Jonathan and Rachel,
whenever they could,
would spend time together.
They would take long walks
in the hills,
and they would talk,
sometimes about peace
between the Jews and the gentiles,
and whether it was worthwhile
raising families during
terrible times like these,
but mostly they would talk
about the things they liked to do
and about nature—
the beauty of sunsets,
the wonder of trees—
and about ideas—
good and evil,
free will and destiny,
and whether God,
whom they loved,
really existed.

One afternoon during a walk,
they watched a hare
darting and hopping
until it disappeared into a cave
with a low entrance,
hidden by shrubs
and undiscovered.
With excitement,
they crawled inside.
Jonathan kissed the girl.
They took off their clothing
and Jonathan lay down in the cave,
the beautiful girl beside him,
and for the first time,
they each experienced
the joy of love.

From that day on
they met secretly in that cave
as often as they could,
and their passion for each other grew.
Jonathan loved Rachel,
and she became
the bride of his youth,
and he cared for her.
And she loved him and cared for him.

As for Eleazar and John,
they each possessed one or two girls
before choosing brides for themselves,
and Simon possessed a few.

145

As for Judah Maccabee,
although countless women wanted him,
and he could have possessed any,
and he did possess many,
he did not take one for a bride.
For he was obsessed with Israel,
and she alone possessed him.

Mattathias's Last Deeds

Mattathias and the men loyal to him
went about pulling down altars
along the coast
and within the borders of Israel.
Whenever they found
uncircumcised Jewish boys,
they circumcised them
in defiance of the king's decree.

And whenever they found brave men
who wanted to join them,
they welcomed them.

During the course of one year,
Mattathias's work went well.
He even recovered some Torah scrolls
saved by the hands of righteous gentiles,
who helped the Jews
rescue the religion of their ancestors
from the hands of the king.
Thus did a few good men

attempt to prevent
the triumph of evil.

The Death of Mattathias

At the end of that year,
Mattathias grew weak
and knew he was going to die.
He called his sons
to his bedside
and said,
"Your bravery and righteousness
have only grown stronger
during this time
of persecution and destruction,
and your anger
has been transformed
into righteous indignation.

"Now, my sons,
the time has come
when you must realize
that the fight for Torah
and righteousness
never comes to an end.
We must fight the good fight
our whole lives through,
from generation to generation.
And you must be willing
to give up your lives—

147

if give them up you must—
fighting for the sake of the Covenant
between the Creator
and our fathers.

"Always remember
the deeds of our ancestors.
Do that,
and you shall distinguish yourselves
and receive honor and glory,
and your names shall live
forever.

"Was not Abraham faithful
in spite of his terrible ordeal
during the binding of Isaac
his son?
And did he not show kindness
and give hospitality generously
to strangers?
And did he not try to save the lives
of the good people
in Sodom?

"Did not Jacob
wrestle with the Almighty
and thereby earn
the surname of Israel—
'wrestler with God'?
And did he not become
father of the children of Israel
and of the House of Jacob?

148

"Did not David,
in spite of unforgivable sins,
ask forgiveness
of the merciful and loving
Creator?
And was he not forgiven?
And for never-ending
perseverance, devotion, and valor,
did he not inherit the throne
of an everlasting kingdom?

"And was not Elijah,
for showing purest faith,
swept up by a whirlwind
and carried bodily into heaven?

"By these examples,
we learn from generation
to generation
that those who put their trust
in Heaven
shall not be overcome.

"Learn to recognize the words
of the evil man.
Those who follow him
are deceived
and like sheep are led
to the land of the dead.

"The evil man says,
'There is only one way,

and I have it!
There is only one truth,
and I know it!'
Know him, too, by the bitter hatred
in his heart—
by the contempt he shows
for those who disagree,
by his intolerance.
He does not treat people
with respect or dignity.
He insults them,
degrades them,
humiliates them,
and calls them names.

"His conditional love
enslaves men's hearts
and minds and souls.
And he will break
every promise he makes.

"He is harsh and solemn,
severe and joyless.
He hates the world
with its pleasures
and would destroy it
if he could.
He does not laugh
or sing or dance,
and scorns those who do.

"The righteous man,
the good man, says:

'Many are the ways
for good people to go.

'Pursue the truth,
but know there is no way
to possess it.

'Be kind and generous,
and respect differences between peoples.
Do not try to make them
all the same.

'Enjoy life
and encourage others to do likewise.
Live and let live!
That is the way to show respect.
That is the road to peace.'

"Fight intolerance.
It is the root of all evil.

"Serve and defend
the weak among you—
orphans, widows,
strangers, slaves, and servants,
the infirm, the old,
women, and the poor.

"Fight for justice
and fight for liberty.
Resist tyranny.

"Do these things
and you shall win glory
for yourselves and your people,
and you shall be a light to the world.

"My boys,
no father has ever had better sons—
no father since the world began.
You have been a source
of pride, comfort, and joy
to me and your mother—
whom we remember and still love—
since the days
when you were born."
The dying old man's eyes
filled with tears.
He composed himself
and resumed.

"Now these are my wishes:
Simon Thassi,
you are wise
and also a man of common sense.
My sons,
always listen
to your brother Simon
as you have listened to me.
He shall advise you like a father.

"Judah Maccabee,
you have been a warrior,
mighty and brave,
from your youth.

Remarkable is your talent for this.
My sons,
let your brother Judah
be your leader
in fighting the battles of our people.

"Accept in your company
anyone who keeps the Torah
and anyone who is righteous,
and avenge the wrongs
done to your people.
Pay back in full
all remorseless acts of evil.

"Finally,
follow the commandments.
They are a divine gift to our people."

Then Mattathias
blessed his five sons.
And in the 146th year
of the Kingdom of the Greeks,   [166 B.C.E.]
Mattathias was gathered
to his fathers.

His sons buried him
in the tomb of his ancestors
in Modin.
The trumpet sounded,
"Ta RA, ta RA, ta RAA."

And the people chanted words of the prophet:
"Holy, holy, holy is YHV
of the hosts.
The whole earth is full of his glory."

All Israel
went into mourning
and lamentation
for many days.

And the people chanted,
"All flesh is grass,
and all the goodliness thereof
is as the flower of the field.
The grass withers,
the flower fades
when the breath of YHV
passes over it.
Surely the people is grass.
The grass withers,
the flower fades,
but the word of our God
stands forever."

BALLAD 5
JUDAH MACCABEE

Judah Maccabee Takes His Father's Place

The sons of a great man
rarely live up to him,
but the five sons of Mattathias did.
And some even surpassed him.

Four sons turned to the fifth,
to their brother Simon,
just as their father
had told them to do.

Simon said to them,
"Brothers, the children of Israel
are besieged on all sides
by enemies who hate them,
and in Judea,
even among our own people,
are enemies who hate us.
But the Almighty has provided us
with the greatest of warriors and leaders
to overcome them—
our very own brother,
Judah Maccabee."

Thereupon
four brothers looked to the fifth—
to Judah Maccabee—
just as their brother Simon
told them to do.

And Judah, the son of Mattathias,
the one called Maccabee,
stood up and took his father's place.

And his brothers,
who had stood by their father,
now stood up proudly
by Judah Maccabee,
who was willing to fight
the battles of Israel.

His brothers kissed him,
embraced him, and cheered him.

The Origin of *Maccabee*

Some say
the surname Maccabee
comes from the Hebrew word for "hammer,"
for Judah pounded the enemy repeatedly,
striking rhythmically and relentlessly
and with an irresistible force.

Soon we shall see
how he overthrew Syrian generals
in quick succession,
all pounded like so many nails
under the Hammer—
under Maccabee.

Others say
he was called the Hammer
because the helmet he wore
looked like a hammer's head.

Still others say
that Judah,
from the time he was a little boy,
shouted "Maccabee!"
whenever he accomplished
something he considered wonderful,
and that "Maccabee"
stands for words of Torah
that mean
"Who is like you, YHV, among the gods?"

מי כמכה באלם יהוה

Mee	Ckhah-mo-ckhah	Bah-ay-leem,	YHV?
M	C	B	Y*

---

*The letters MCBY are the transliterated initials of the first four
Hebrew words of Exodus 15:11 and form an acronym. With the
appropriate vowels added, MCBY becomes "Maccabee."

Judah Maccabee Prepares for Battle

Judah Maccabee
was the body and soul
of the Jewish people.
From the instant he took
his father's place,
he spent every waking moment
serving them.
He had little life apart from Israel.

Judah Maccabee
was a genius in warfare.
He fought campaigns for freedom
and was the salvation of his people.
He brought honor to the Jews
and restored their former glory.

Judah Maccabee
was full of grace,
whether in motion or perfectly still,
and people stared at him in admiration.
Whether standing or sitting
or even sound asleep,
he had great dignity
and a commanding demeanor.
And his speech carried authority.

When he prepared for battle,
he put on full armor—
a coat of mail, a breastplate, and a helmet—
and he belted on a sword
to defend and protect his people.

158

Maccabee looked taller than he was,
and when going forth to battle,
he looked like a giant.

Judah fought like a young lion,
and when he shouted,
it was like this ferocious beast
roaring in hunger for prey,
for he pursued and destroyed
the oppressors of his people.
The wicked shrank
at the mention of his name.
They were dismayed,
and they were afraid.

He brought grief to many kings,
but the House of Jacob
was gladdened by his deeds.
All of Israel remembers him
even today,
and blesses him forever.

He went through the towns
and cities of Judea,
destroying evil wherever he found it,
deflecting violence against Israel,
and rallying those without hope.
And his fame
reached the ends of the earth.

Maccabee Battles Apollonius

Apollonius, a Greek general,
was determined to root out
the religion of the Jews
and the Jews themselves.
He raised a great army
of gentiles from Samaria
to make war on Israel.

Among the nations,
the government paid the soldiers,
for they were professional warriors
whose goal was conquest—
invasion, followed by assimilation
or annihilation.

But when Judah Maccabee
went forth with a band of Jewish men,
his "army" consisted of volunteers—
farmers, shepherds, workmen, scholars—
young men fighting for liberty,
for the ways of their ancestors,
for their right to exist.

Maccabee and Apollonius
engaged in battle.
In the first encounter
Maccabee killed Apollonius.
Judah's men slew most of the enemy,
and the survivors fled.

Judah's men shouted,
"Maccabee!"

Judah smiled;
then, turning toward heaven,
he cried,
"Maccabee!"

And his men shouted
over and over again,
"Maccabee!"
"Maccabee!"
"Maccabee!"

Judah bent down
and picked up Apollonius's sword
and examined it.
This sword was famous
as the finest in the world.
Now Maccabee would fight with it
for the rest of his life.

Maccabee Battles Seron

Seron, a commander
of the Syrian army,
said to himself,
"I will make a name for myself
and win glory,
for I will fight and kill

Judah Maccabee
and all who despise the king's decree."

Judah was ascending
the road that leads to Beth-Horon.
He looked down
and saw the enemy
on the plain below.

His men said,
"How can we who are so few
fight against so many?
Look at them!
How well-fed they are,
while we go hungry."

Maccabee replied,
"The lean fight better than the fat.
And it is not hard for the few
to fight the many and win—
if Heaven is on our side.

"Besides,
victory in battle does not depend
so much on numbers
as on strength and courage
and good sense.
We have them all,
and these are gifts
that come from Heaven.

"Our enemies approach,
filled with violence,

arrogance, and iniquity.
They are intent on destroying us—
taking our lives
and our women and children as slaves.

"They invade
to subjugate and destroy us,
even though they know
they have no cause—
for we have done them no harm.

"By contrast,
we fight for our lives
and for the things
we believe in!
Our cause is just,
our cause is right.
And with Heaven's help,
we shall overcome them.
So your concern
is unfounded."

Then Maccabee prayed
in the words of David:
"God is our refuge
and our strength,
an ever-present help in trouble.
We have nothing to fear
though the earth should change,
though the mountains shake
in the heart of the sea,
though its waters roar and foam."

Then Maccabee and his band
raced from the mountain
down to the plain,
pounced on the Syrian enemy,
and crushed them in an instant.

Judah's men shouted,
"Maccabee!"

Judah smiled;
then, turning toward heaven,
he cried,
"Maccabee!"

And his men shouted
over and over again,
"Maccabee!"
"Maccabee!"
"Maccabee!"

Antiochus Epiphanes Ruins His Economy

Israel was surrounded on all sides
by hostile nations.
But after the battle with Seron,
fear of Maccabee and his brothers
seized those nations.

Judah Maccabee's fame
reached Antiochus Epiphanes

as he sat on the throne in Antioch,
for the whole world
was talking about Judah
and his skill in warfare.

When Antiochus heard the news,
he sent for all the warriors of Syria
to come together
for the purpose of invading Judea,
and he gathered
one of the largest armies ever assembled.

Then he opened his treasury,
paid the soldiers a full year's wages,
and ordered them to be ready
the moment he needed them.

No sooner had he done this
than he was informed
that the treasury
was now depleted.

His advisors raised questions
about his expenses:

"My lord and my god,
how do you intend to pay
the army *next* year?"

"How are you going to pay
your servants and advisors *this* year?"

"How are you going
to go on giving the lavish gifts
you are so fond of giving?"

"How, my lord and my god,
do you intend to pay your bills?"

And one was even
so bold as to say:
"Once you were the wealthiest king
on the face of the earth,
wealthier by far than any other king
who ever lived!
But today,
the economy is in ruins!"

Thereupon
Antiochus Epiphanes,
"God Manifest to Men"
and the "Light of the World,"
devised a scheme
to replenish the treasury.
He would go to Persia
to collect tributes from that country—
and from any other country
that would pay.

Lysias Becomes Regent

Antiochus Epiphanes
appointed as regent
his dear friend Lysias,
a man of royal blood,
to rule the kingdom of Syria
while he was away
chasing after wealth.
Lysias would oversee
the king's business
from the Euphrates River
to the Egyptian border.

Antiochus instructed Lysias
to raise and educate
and train in warfare
little Antiochus,
his son,
until the time he returned
with mountains of money
and infinite glory.

Antiochus Epiphanes
assigned to Lysias
half his army and all his elephants.
He put him in charge of everything,
and this is what he told him to do:
to use the army
to crush the Jews of Judea and Jerusalem,
to root out and destroy
the strength of Israel

167

and any remnant in Jerusalem,
and to completely annihilate the Jews—
to make them vanish forever
like footprints in the sand.

As for Jerusalem,
Lysias was to blot out forever
all memories of her
as a Jewish city.
He was to place gentiles
in all quarters of the city,
divide up the land into parcels,
and assign them by lot
to his officers.

Then, in the 147th year
of the Kingdom of the Greeks,
Antiochus Epiphanes
took half his army,
departed from Antioch,
and crossed the Syrian border.

And when he came
to the river Euphrates,
he crossed it
and marched
into the high countries.

BALLAD 6
MACCABEE'S GREAT VICTORY

Preparation for the Battle at Emmaus

As soon as Lysias assumed power,
he called upon three generals:
Ptolemy, whose father was Dorymenes,
Nicanor,
and Gorgias—
the three greatest warriors
among Antiochus's friends.
He gave them orders to gather
forty thousand foot soldiers
and seven thousand men on horseback
to invade Judea and destroy it,
just as the king had commanded.

All the strength of Syria
and all the strength of Philistia
joined together
to form that mighty army.

It was just as
the prophet had said:
"Behold, and see!
A people comes

from the north country,
a great nation stirring
from the distant reaches of the earth.
They brandish bow and spear.
They are cruel and without mercy.
Their voice is like the sound
of the roaring sea.
They ride upon horses
in battle formation
against you,
O daughter of Zion!"

The three generals
went forth with all that might
until they came
to the town of Emmaus,
located on the plain.
And outside the town
they pitched their camp.

Some merchants of Judea—
Jewish converts and gentiles—
on seeing the size
of that great army,
fully expected it to defeat
the faithful Jews.
So they took silver and gold in abundance,
and other great riches besides,
and came into the gentile camp
to make arrangements in advance
to buy the children of Israel
as slaves.

When Maccabee and his brothers
saw how greatly multiplied
was the misery of the Jews
and saw all those enemy forces
encamped within their borders,
they knew the king had given orders
to completely destroy the Jews.

Maccabee said to his brothers,
"The time has come
to turn things around—
to end our ruination
and restore our former glory."

Then all the young men of Israel
gathered together to prepare for battle
and pray,

"Have mercy on us, O Holy One,
according to your steadfast love.
Turn from fierce anger,
and show us mercy and compassion,
as you swore to our fathers.

"For Jerusalem is laid waste,
the City of David is like a desert,
and none of her children goes in or out.
The Temple is trampled upon.
Our enemies hold the Citadel,
and live in Jerusalem
or pass through it with ease.

171

"All joy is gone
from the House of Jacob.
There is no music, no dancing.
The flute and the harp are silent."

The young men of Israel
assembled in Mizpeh,
just north of Jerusalem.
There was a time long ago
when the men of Israel
prayed in Mizpeh
with songs of gladness,
when they beheld Saul,
their first king,
for the first time.
But now the people fasted,
put on sackcloth,
smudged ashes on their brows,
and rent their clothing.

They brought with them
an intact Torah scroll,
one that the enemy had captured
but had not torn up and burned.
With great joy and excitement
they carefully unrolled the scroll,
only to find that the gentiles
had drawn on the parchment
pictures of Greek gods!
Icons of idols!
So they cried out to Heaven,
saying,

"What are we to do with this?
Why did we bother to bring it?
Where are we to dispose of it?

"Your Holy Scriptures
are desecrated!
The Temple
is trampled upon and polluted!
Your priests
are humiliated and in mourning!

"Behold and see
how great is the gentile army
that now comes to destroy us.
What things they imagine about us
only you, O God, can know.
How can we make a stand against them
unless you are our help?"

When they finished praying,
they sounded the trumpets,
"Ta RA, ta RA, ta RAA."

Then Maccabee appointed officers
over the people.
As for the men
engaged to be married
or occupied in building homes
or in planting vineyards—
or too frightened to go to battle—
these he discharged,

ordering them to return to their homes
in accordance with the teachings
of Torah.

Victory at Emmaus

Then Maccabee and his men
marched toward Emmaus
and encamped just south of the city.

Maccabee addressed his men.
"Men of Israel!
Brace yourselves!
Tomorrow at dawn
we fight a great fight!
Standing before us
is a mighty army
made up of many nations
who have come together
for the sole purpose
of destroying us
because we are Jews.

"It is better to die in battle
than to witness the destruction
of our people and our Temple.

"Men of Israel,
the Creator's will is in heaven.
Let the Creator's will be done!"

Gorgias, the enemy's commanding general,
took five thousand infantry
and one thousand of his best cavalry
and left camp under cover of night
to storm the camp of the Jews
and take them by surprise.

Judah learned of the plan,
and he and his men
left camp early that night.

When Gorgias came
into Maccabee's camp,
he was surprised to find
no one there.
"The Jews have escaped!
They have fled to the mountains!
Let's hunt for them there!"

At daybreak, Judah appeared on the plain
with three thousand men
poorly armed because of their poverty.
Instead of helmets
they wore hoods;
instead of brandishing swords
they carried knives.
They looked at the enemy camp
and saw that it was strong—
with helmet and armor and sword,
and cavalry ready for battle,
already patrolling—
an army well prepared for war.

Maccabee said to his men,
"Men of Israel!
Do not fear their great numbers.
This is the turning point—
the critical moment
we've been waiting for—
the time to recover our liberty
and to regain a happy life
or else to suffer a disgraceful fate
by allowing our people
to come to an end.

"Fight valiantly for freedom,
the same freedom
loved by all men
who dwell beneath the stars of heaven,
but by you above all.

"Death comes to everyone,
even to cowards,
even to those who do not fight.
But if you fight now
and if you die now,
you do so for freedom—
freedom of religion,
freedom of country,
and freedom of soul.
And you will win everlasting glory.

"Remember how our ancestors
were delivered at the Red Sea
when Pharaoh's army pursued them.

"Now, let us pray to Heaven
that the Almighty
will be as gracious to us
as he was to our ancestors,
that he will bestow
his merciful favor upon us
and help us destroy the enemy
that comes to enslave or murder us
just because we are Jews.
Let the world know
there is a God
who delivers and saves Israel!"

The enemy looked up
and saw Maccabee and his troops
coming toward them.
So they went forth from their camp
to meet them.

From Maccabee's side
came the trumpet charge,
"RA ta ta, RA ta ta, RA ta ta, TAA."
Then came the attack.

The two sides engaged,
and the fighting was fierce.
There was great carnage of gentiles—
the very opposite of their expectations,
because the Jews were outnumbered
and poorly armed.

The enemy became so frightened
that they fled across the plain,
many dropping their swords
as they ran.

Maccabee's men pursued them
and, as they chased, stooped down
to pick up the enemy swords.
So the last of the fleeing soldiers
were cut down
by their very own weapons.

Those who escaped
fled to the city of Gezer
or to the plains of Idumea
or to the towns of Ashdod and Jabneh,
with Maccabee's men
close behind.
Three thousand of the enemy
died that day.

Then Judah and his men
returned to camp.
Maccabee said,
"Brave men of Judea,
you have fought gloriously.
But we still have one more battle to fight.
Gorgias's troops are in the mountains,
not far off, and they surely
are planning to attack.
So be prepared.
Stand your ground
and you will overcome them.

And after that victory is won,
you can take all the spoils you like."

Even as Maccabee spoke,
a detachment
of enemy soldiers appeared,
looking down from the mountain.
They were astonished
at what they saw.
A small company
of poorly armed Jews
had put their army to flight
and was now burning their tents.
The smoke told the whole story.

The enemy soldiers on the mountain
were very much afraid.
Terror struck their hearts
and threw their minds
into confusion.

On seeing Maccabee's troops
on the plain, so pitifully equipped
and yet so eager to fight,
they scattered and fled
into foreign lands.

Judah Maccabee was standing
in the middle of his men.
In amazement
he watched the enemy flee
without a fight.

Suddenly
Maccabee's men
began to applaud and shout.

They rushed toward Judah.
They pushed and shoved
and crushed one another
as they tried to touch him,
to embrace him, to kiss him.
They lifted him high
upon their shoulders
and carried him aloft,
clapping and cheering,
singing and dancing
with great cries of joy,
shouting over and over again,
"Maccabee!
Maccabee!
Maccabee!"

Judah gazed fondly at his men.
Then he turned to heaven,
and with tears rolling down his cheeks,
he cried,
"Maccabee!"

When the excitement
of victory subsided,
Maccabee's men
plundered the enemy camp
filled with treasure—
much silver and gold,

beautiful blue silk and purple fabrics
dyed by the murex of the sea,
and other great riches besides,
which the wealthy
and powerful merchants
had brought
as payment in advance
for their Jewish slaves.

The enemy captains
gave Lysias a full report
of the bravery of Maccabee's soldiers,
and how nobly they were ready
to die for freedom,
and of their great victory.

Lysias became dismayed
and discouraged,
for none of the things
he wanted to happen to Israel
had happened,
and none of the things
the king had commanded him to do
had come to pass.
So he ordered the army
to retreat to Antioch,
telling his troops
he would return
to crush Judea
another day.

Maccabee and his men
returned home,
singing songs
of liberation and thanksgiving
and praising the Creator:
"I lift up my eyes to the hills.
From whence does my help come?
My help comes from YHV,
who made heaven and earth. . . .
The holy one who keeps Israel
neither slumbers nor sleeps."

"O give thanks to YHV,
who is good,
and whose mercy
endures forever."

Israel had great deliverance
that day.

Judah Maccabee
turned to his brothers
and said,
"Now is the time
to go up to Jerusalem
and purify
and dedicate the Temple."

BALLAD 7
HANUKAH

Purification of the Temple

The moment Maccabee's men
heard their leader's
amazing announcement,
they closed ranks
and marched up Mount Zion.

When they saw
the Temple
abandoned and neglected,
its altar desecrated,
its gates and doors burned down,
when they saw shrubs and weeds
growing in the courtyards
as in a field or wood
or on a mountainside,
and when they saw
the chambers of the priests torn down,
Maccabee's men rent their clothes.
Their eyes welled up with tears,
and they uttered sobs
and cries of lamentation.

They cast ashes on their heads
and fell flat on their faces
upon the ground.

The trumpets sounded the alarm—
"RA ta ta, RA ta ta, RA ta ta, TAA."
That great call
could have wakened the dead.
It reached to heaven
and stirred the people to action.

Maccabee assigned men
to fight the enemy in the Citadel.
Then his thoughts turned
completely to the Temple.

He appointed priests
of the highest character
to purify the sacred place
and haul out the polluted stones.

Judah and his brothers
then deliberated on what to do
about the defiled altar
of burnt offerings.
This was the altar on which
the gentiles and the converts
had sacrificed swine to Zeus.

They decided to tear it down,
lest it be a constant reminder
of the desecration.

No sooner
had they knocked it down
than Maccabee realized
this was the same altar
that Zerubbabel had built,
the same altar
that the Almighty had commanded
Cyrus to build—
Cyrus, that great and righteous gentile,
king of the Persians and Medes.

It was Cyrus who had liberated the Jews
from their captivity in Babylon
and had led them in their march
back to Jerusalem,
Cyrus whom the Almighty
called "my shepherd,"
Cyrus whom the Almighty
called "my anointed"
and charged with the rebuilding
of his House in Jerusalem.

So Maccabee was in a quandary.
Had he erred
in tearing down the altar
defiled by evil gentiles?
For that same altar
had been built
through the goodness
of righteous gentiles
at the command of God!

And those stones, even if defiled,
were holy, too!

So he ordered that the stones
be carried out and carefully piled up
in a special place
on the Temple Mount,
until such time as a prophet
would arise once more in Israel
and tell them what to do.

Then the Jews gathered new, whole stones,
according to the Torah,
and built a new altar
with the same design as the old.

They repaired the Temple
and restored things
within the sanctuary
and sanctified them
together with the Temple courts.

They made new sacred vessels—
a new seven-branched lampstand,
an incense altar,
and a table for the ceremonial bread—
and they set them all up.

They decorated the Temple facade
with gold crowns and shields,
and they hung new doors
upon the gates
and on the entrances to the chambers.

They made fire
by striking flint stones.
Then they burned incense on the altar
and lit the seven-branched lampstand
to give light within the Temple.

They set loaves on the table.
And with the hanging of the curtains,
they completed all the work
they had set about to do.

Three years earlier
the gentiles had desecrated
the Temple and the altar,
and all of Israel
had gone into mourning.

Now the restored Temple
with its new altar
was to be dedicated with joy—
with the singing of songs
accompanied by musical instruments—
the people remembering
how just a few weeks before
they had celebrated
the festival of Sukkot
while wandering
in the hills and mountains
and living in caves
like wild animals.

The First Hanukah:
The Festival of Dedication

In the late afternoon,
before the sun went down
signaling the start of the new day,
the people had gathered
on the Temple Mount.
And by sunset
at the start of the twenty-fifth day
of the month of Kislev
in the 148th year
of the Kingdom of the Greeks,   [164 B.C.E.]
all of Jerusalem
had gathered on the Mount
to dedicate the Temple
and the new altar of burnt offerings.

Directly in front of the Temple
was the inner courtyard,
called the Court of Israel.
A gate led from the courtyard landing
to fifteen steps
down to an orchestra in the first portion
of the outer courtyard,
called the Court of the Women.

As they used to do
for the festival of Sukkot,
they had set up colossal lampstands
in the Court of the Women.

188

Each lampstand
had a great columnar stem
bearing four gigantic golden bowls.
Each lamp bowl was filled to capacity
with fifteen gallons of oil
and held a giant wick
made from the breeches of priests.

At the base of each lampstand
were four ladders,
each leading to a lamp bowl.
Youths aspiring to the priesthood
had climbed those ladders
while holding large jars of oil,
which they poured into the bowls.
There they waited expectantly
for the signal to light the lamps.

On the festival of Sukkot
the courtyard lamps burned
only for the first night,
but for this new holiday
the lamps would be lighted every night
for eight consecutive nights!

The dedication ceremony began
just as the sun went down,
when priests blew trumpets.

Then a musician played
a melody on the flute.

Then a priest chanted,
"We bless you
from the house of YHV.
God is YHV,
who has given us light."

And another priest
chanted from the Torah,
"And God said, 'Let there be light!'
And there was light."

Then the priests
blew trumpet fanfares,
and in the twilight,
the young men on ladders
lit the giant lamps
and flooded the courtyards with light.
As darkness continued to fall,
the light became so bright
that it illuminated all of Jerusalem!
There was not a courtyard
in the entire city
that did not reflect that light.

Trumpets sounded again,
louder than before.

Then a priest
chanted from the Torah:
"Hear, O Israel,
YHV is our God,
YHV alone!"

And the people responded:
"Hear, O Israel,
YHV is our God,
YHV alone!"

Then the choir sang,
"Make joyful sounds to YHV,
all the earth!
Serve YHV with gladness!"

The musicians standing on the staircase
between the courts
began to play harps, lutes, and cymbals,
while in the gateway
on the upper landing,
two priests again blew trumpets.

The choir chanted the psalm
for the dedication of the Temple:

"I will extol you, O YHV,
for you have lifted me up,
and have not let my enemies
rejoice over me. . . .

"O YHV, you brought up my soul
from the underworld
and restored me to life
from among those
who went down to the grave. . . .

"God's anger is but for a moment,
while God's favor is for a lifetime.
Weeping may come in the evening,
but joy comes in the morning. . . .

"You turned my mourning
into dancing.
You took off my sackcloth
and covered me with joy. . . .

"O YHV, my God,
I will give thanks to you forever."

Then, in the orchestra,
young women
carrying wands wreathed with ivy
and waving olive branches
and palm fronds
marched in processional
and began to dance as they passed
from the orchestra
into the Court of the Women
to the sound of trumpets.

And then young men
selected for their good deeds
ran and danced
and did somersaults
with flaming torches in their hands!

The jubilation exceeded anything
ever seen anywhere at any other time.
Anyone who did not see the rejoicing

of the ceremony of light
on that very first Hanukah night
has not seen rejoicing!

When the dancing ended,
the people fell on their faces
and worshiped and gave prayers
of thanksgiving and praise
to the Creator,
who had given them
such success and such joy.

The choir sang a psalm
of thanksgiving:

"O give thanks to YHV,
who is good,
and whose steadfast love
endures forever. . . .

"I shall not die but live
and declare the works of YHV.
YHV has chastened me greatly,
but has not given me over to death. . . .

"I give thanks to you
for you have answered me
and have become my salvation.
The stone that the builders rejected
has become the chief cornerstone.
This is YHV's doing;
it is marvelous in our eyes.

"This is the day that YHV has made.
Let us rejoice and be glad in it.

"We beseech you, O YHV!
Hosanna!
We beseech you, O YHV!
May you let us now prosper!"

A priest read from the Torah:
"I am YHV your God,
who brought you out of the land of Egypt,
out of the house of bondage."

Judah Maccabee and his brothers
had invited
the righteous gentiles among them
to join in the celebration
and to be honored—
gentiles who,
at great risk to their lives,
had hidden in their homes
Torahs and scholars of Torah
and circumcised babies
when the inspectors came by
to inspect Jewish homes.

When Maccabee and his brothers
set out to honor Cyrus
and all the righteous gentiles,
most of the priests and elders objected,
but there was no high priest
to resolve the dispute.

194

Maccabee quickly prevailed,
for Judah Maccabee
was then everything
to the children of Israel.

So all the people
sang the praises of David,
the everlasting king,
who conceived of the Temple,
and of Solomon, his son, who built it,
and of Cyrus, the righteous gentile,
whom the Almighty
commanded to rebuild it.

And the choir sang,

"My House shall be called
a house of prayer for all peoples."

"Let the peoples give thanks
to you, O God!
O let the peoples be glad
and sing for joy,
for you judge all peoples equally
and are the guide
for all the peoples upon the earth."

Then the young men lit torches
from the Temple court lamps.
And bearing the torches,
they marched in procession
down the Temple Mount

to Jerusalem below.
They continued
down the streets of the city,
where they lit all the lamps
on the doorways
of every home.

This was a time of great joy
for the people of Israel
and the righteous gentiles
who dwelled among them.
For all the shameful things
that the wicked had done
had been washed or cast away.

Maccabee and his brothers
and the whole congregation of Israel
ordained that the Festival of Dedication
should be celebrated for eight days
at this season every year,
beginning the twenty-fifth day of Kislev.
And the festival was to be kept
with joy and gladness.

The people dedicated a new altar,
and they rededicated the Temple.
But most important of all,
they rededicated their lives
to liberty, righteousness, and justice,
and to the quest
for everlasting peace.

And the choir sang
these words of David:

"The heavens are YHV's,
but God has given the earth
to the children of Adam."

"Praise YHV, all nations!
Extol God, all peoples!
For God's love for mankind is great,
and the faithfulness of YHV
endures forever.
Hallelujah!"

The celebration went on
all through the night.

The next morning,
at dawn of that first day,
the priests made sacrifice
upon the new altar of burnt offerings
according to the commandments.

And that night,
as the night before,
and for all those eight marvelous nights,
the whole city of Jerusalem
was ablaze with lights.

BALLAD 8
BATTLES IN GALILEE AND GILEAD

Resolve of the Gentiles

With the inauguration
of the Festival of Dedication,
the Jews reestablished their right
to worship God in the Temple.
But hostility toward them
did not cease.

And so
when the celebration of the holiday
was over,
the children of Israel went to work
to rebuild upon Mount Zion
high walls with strong towers,
lest the hostile gentiles round about
come and tear everything down
as they had done before.

When the nations round about
heard that the Temple
had been dedicated anew
and restored to its former glory,
they became agitated.

They began to think of ways
to destroy the Jews in the Diaspora,
those living among them
and under their rule.

As the psalmist said,
"Behold!
They lie in wait to kill me;
arrogant men band themselves
against me
for no sin of mine
and no transgression.
O YHV,
through no fault of mine,
they run and make ready.
Rouse yourself!
Come to my help and see!
O YHV,
you are God of all,
God of Israel.
Awake, and punish
all the nations
who treacherously plot evil!"

Maccabee Fights On

When the wicked sons of Esau,
who lived in Idumea,
attacked Israel,
Maccabee defeated them.

He did not forget
the evil inflicted
by the men of Baean,
who had set traps
on lonely roads,
ambushing and massacring
unarmed Jewish men,
women, and children.

Maccabee pursued
and captured these men,
then locked them in towers
and set the towers on fire.

He fought many battles
and won them all.
And after taking the town of Jazer
and the villages around it,
he returned to Jerusalem.

The gentiles in the land of Gilead
were determined to destroy
the Jews living within their borders.
On learning this, the Jews fled
to the fortress of Dathema,
where they sent letters to Judah,
saying,

"The gentiles with whom
we've lived for so long
in friendship and in peace
have suddenly turned on us

200

and decided to destroy us.
They have raised an army,
and their general
is named Timothy.
They are preparing
to take the Dathema fortress,
where we are taking refuge.

"Many in Gilead are already slain.
All Jewish males in the land of Tob
have been put to death.
Their wives and children
have been carried off as slaves.
Come as quickly as you can
to save us."

Judah was still reading this letter
when a messenger came
from Galilee, reporting,
"The gentiles in the cities
of Acre, Tyre, Sidon,
and all the cities and towns of Galilee
have united to annihilate the Jews."

Judah said to his brother,
"Simon, you attack
the towns of Galilee
and bring the refugees back to Judea,
while Jonathan and I attack
the towns of Gilead,
gather the refugees there,
and bring them home."

Then he appointed Azarias
and Joseph ben Zechariah
as captains, whose job it was
to defend the people in Judea,
and he left them
a small army.
"You are in charge.
Stay in the garrisons and defend them.
Under no circumstances
take it upon yourselves to start a battle
while I am away."

Then Judah assigned Simon
three thousand troops
to take into Galilee,
while he and Jonathan
took eight thousand men
into Gilead.

Victories in Galilee and Gilead

Simon marched into Galilee
and won many battles there.
Then he led the Jews of Galilee
and all they possessed
joyfully into Judea.

During this time,
Judah and Jonathan crossed the Jordan
and were marching in the desert

when they encountered Nabateans,
Arabs on the side of the Jews.

The Arabs told Maccabee
all that had happened
to the Jews in Gilead.
Many had been locked up
in fortresses in Bosor, Alema,
Chaspho, Maked,
Karnaim, and other cities, too.

Maccabee said to the Nabateans,
"Rest assured,
tomorrow we intend to storm
every one of those places
and rescue the Jews in the fortresses,
then destroy the cities—
all of them in one day."

But Maccabee
did not wait for tomorrow.
He immediately turned toward the desert,
to the city of Bosor.
He stormed it,
killed the men by the edge of the sword,
released all the Jews,
then burned down the fortress
and the city, too.

That night Maccabee moved on.
Near the city of Alema,
he made camp.

Just as dawn began to break,
he awoke to see an amazing sight.
His men were already up and about,
bearing ladders and engines of war.
The siege had already begun!

When Judah saw this, he grinned.
For his men had let him sleep,
and they had proceeded without him.
They had carried out his orders
without waiting to hear them.

The rams' horns sounded the alarm,
"RA ta ta, RA ta ta, RA ta ta, TAA."
The enemy came pouring
out of the city ready to fight.

Judah's men advanced
in three battalions,
trumpets sounding
as Judah marched behind.

Timothy, realizing
this had to be Maccabee,
fled with his army.

Judah ordered some troops
to release the Jews
imprisoned in the fortress
while he gave chase,
smote the enemy,
and slaughtered them.

Maccabee then turned
to the city of Maspha.
He stormed and conquered it,
killed all the males,
took all the spoils,
released the Jews
imprisoned in the fortress,
then burned the city
to the ground.

After Maspha,
Judah moved on,
taking Chaspho, Maked,
and all the cities of Gilead,
one right after the other.

The Battle at Karnaim

After Judah Maccabee
conquered these cities
and released the Jews,
he marched toward Karnaim.

Timothy, the enemy general,
had raised yet another army
and pitched camp
below the city of Raphon,
near a mountain stream
swollen with melting winter snow—
turbulent, torrential, and treacherous.

Maccabee sent spies
toward the enemy camp.
They returned with this report:
"All the gentiles living round about
have gathered a great army
with Timothy in command.
He has recruited regulars
and also hired Arab mercenaries.
The soldiers have pitched their tents
on the other side of the river,
but they are prepared to cross it
and attack us."

Judah walked toward the river.

When Timothy saw Maccabee
coming in his direction,
he called his officers and said,
"When Maccabee reaches
the riverbank,
he will stop to inspect the torrent.
Should he cross it,
we cannot withstand him
and he will prevail against us.
But if he is frightened by the river
and remains on the other side,
then we shall cross it
and engage him in battle."

When Maccabee reached the river,
he studied it.
Then he gave his captains these orders:

206

"Stay here and keep the refugees
on this side of the river.
As for the fighting men,
tell them I order every man of them
to cross the river and fight!"

Then Maccabee jumped into the river.
He was the first.
On seeing him reach the other side,
his troops followed.

The gentiles were thrown
into disarray.
They cast down their arms
and fled into Karnaim,
where there was a temple
with a great idol.
They ran into the temple,
seeking protection from the god.

Maccabee and his army
followed in swift pursuit.
They captured Karnaim
and released the Jews.
Then they burned down the temple
with the soldiers in it.

Judah Maccabee seemed invincible.

207

BALLAD 9
REFUGEES

Maccabee Gathers the Refugees

Judah Maccabee
gathered all the Jews he had set free
and the many more
who had been forced to flee
from their homes in Gilead—
the land where Jews
had dwelled for generations,
the land where Elijah the prophet
was born and lived,
where he wandered and preached.

Maccabee gathered them all,
the great and the small,
the rich and the poor,
the healthy and the sick,
the community leaders and the unknowns,
the shepherds and the scholars,
the young and the old,
all of them with their belongings—
whatever they could carry—
a very great host of refugees.

They began the long march to Judea,
singing as they went
about Elijah the prophet,
Ay-lee-yah-hoo hah-nah-vee:

"Our Elijah—he could see
what God had written—destiny.
So he wandered,
wandered Gilead,
warning men of their iniquity."

Maccabee's goal
was to bring all the refugees
into the land of Judea,
because the land of Gilead
was now ruled by tyrants
who were hostile to Jews,
slaughtering them in droves
or driving them from their homes.

And the refugees sang of Elijah:

"Heaven took him bodily.
Prophet great! Return to me!
Bring Messiah, set us free—
peace on earth eternally!"

As the refugees trudged along,
they came to the city of Ephron,
a great walled city, broad and wide,
nestled between mountains
whose peaks were covered with snow.

Judah was unwilling
to travel the great distance
around the city
over difficult terrain
because of the large numbers
of the weak—
children, the old, and the sick.
So Maccabee headed
straight for Ephron.

When the inhabitants saw all those people
coming toward their city,
they ran and shut the city gates,
and barricaded them
with boulders and rocks.
When Judah saw the gates closing,
he sent a messenger ahead, saying,

"We come in peace.
These are refugees
who have suffered greatly.
We are on our way to Judea.
We only want
to pass through your city,
because many of us are too weak
to walk over the mountains.
We will not harm you."

But the people of Ephron
shouted, "Death to the Jews!"
"Walk through the mountains
and may you all die!"

They refused to open the gates.
So Judah gave orders
for the refugees to pitch their tents
just where they were.

And the refugees sang:

"Our Elijah—he could see
what God had written—destiny.
So he wandered,
wandered Gilead,
warning men of their iniquity."

Maccabee ordered his men to attack.
They besieged Ephron
all day and all night
until the city fell.
Judah killed all the males,
destroyed the city,
and took the spoils.

Then Maccabee and his host
marched through the city,
walking over the dead bodies
of the inhabitants
as they went.

Glory-Seekers

While Maccabee and his host
were marching through Ephron,

Azarias and Joseph ben Zechariah,
captains of the garrisons of Judea,
heard of all the valiant deeds
of Judah, Jonathan, and Simon
in Gilead and Galilee.
So Azarias said to Joseph ben Zechariah,
"Let us make a name for ourselves, too,
by fighting the gentiles nearby."

So they placed two men
in charge of the garrison,
and took two thousand,
and went toward the town of Jamnia
to attack it.

Now it so happened
that Gorgias, the great Syrian general,
was stationed in Jamnia.
When Gorgias saw
the small army of Jews approaching,
he went forth with his mighty army
to engage them in combat.

On seeing Gorgias
and his great army,
Azarias and Joseph ben Zechariah
became terrified
and ordered a hasty retreat,
but not before Gorgias and his men
slaughtered all two thousand.

That day there was a great loss in Israel—
totally needless!—

just because the two men in charge
were disobedient to Maccabee,
envious of him,
and wanted to win a little glory
for themselves.

Maccabee Brings the Refugees Home

From Ephron, the refugees
crossed the river Jordan
onto the great plain
of Beth-Shean.

The refugees were tired,
and there were many stragglers.
Maccabee kept going back to them
and speaking encouraging words,

"We'll soon be there!"

"Keep together!"

"Keep walking!"

"Come along, little guy!
That's the way."

"Young mother there,
you're doing fine!"

"Old father,
here's a walking stick."

"Kinsmen of Elijah,
it's not much longer.
We'll soon be there."

"We're almost home!"

He kept dropping behind
and saying things like this
to keep the stragglers moving.

He would lift up
those unable to continue,
and deliver them
to the strongest of his soldiers,
who then carried them
on their shoulders
all the way
to Jerusalem.

All the host of refugees
whom Maccabee brought
from Galilee and Gilead
went up to Mount Zion in joy
and offered whole burnt offerings,
so glad were they
to arrive safely
in Zion,
in the City of David,
in Jerusalem.

BALLAD 10
THE DEATH OF ANTIOCHUS EPIPHANES

A Disappointed King

While Antiochus Epiphanes
was traveling
through the high countries,
he learned that in Persia
there was a wealthy city called Elymais,
which had treasures of silver and gold
and a very rich temple
that contained splendid tapestries
and a famous relic—
the armor of Alexander the Great.

So Antiochus went to Elymais,
intent on capturing it
and plundering its wealth
and treasure.
He was still hoping
to return to Antioch
with incomparable riches
and glory.

Once more his plan was thwarted,
and his dreams were shattered,
for the people of Elymais
rose up to fight him.
Antiochus Epiphanes fled.

The only thing left for him to do
was to leave Persia.
Perhaps he could yet
fulfill his dreams in Babylon.

Just then a messenger came
with very bad news.
Lysias,
whom Antiochus had placed in power,
and whose armies
were to conquer Judea,
had been routed
and driven from that land.

As for the Jews
whom Lysias was to annihilate,
they were stronger than ever—
even powerful—
for they had acquired many arms
and great wealth from all the spoils
taken from Lysias's armies.

Antiochus also learned
that the Jews
had pulled down the altar
in the Temple of Jerusalem
along with the great image of Zeus—

the one Antiochus himself
had ordered set up.

When the king heard these reports,
he was visibly shaken.
Distressed to the core of his being,
he went to bed,
for he was sick at heart with grief.
Things hadn't turned out
as he had wished.

The "Light of the World" Goes Out

Antiochus Epiphanes,
languishing and despondent,
could barely eat or drink
as his grief continued to grow.
Convinced he was going to die,
he made all the necessary arrangements.

He sent for his friends and said,
"I can no longer sleep at night.
My heart is broken and failing, too.

"How terrible are my afflictions!
How flooded I am with misery!
Only yesterday I had unlimited power
and unlimited riches,
and everyone in my kingdom
loved me—didn't they?"

The truth of the matter was,
they didn't.
Behind his back,
they had long ago stopped calling him
Antiochus Epiphanes.
Instead, they were calling him
Antiochus *Epimanes*—
Antiochus "the Madman."

Antiochus said,
"At last I know
why I'm so horribly afflicted:
It's because
of all the terrible things I did
to the Jews.

"From their Temple in Jerusalem
I stole the vessels of silver and gold,
and I was determined
to annihilate them forever
from the face of the earth.

"Because of these things
all these misfortunes
have befallen me,
and I perish of profound grief,
a stranger in a strange land,
never again to see my palace
and the splendors of my court,
the musicians and the dancing women,
never again to worship
the idols that I love."

Then he sent for Philip,
his dear friend,
and made him regent,
for he was disappointed in Lysias,
whom he called
a fool and a dog,
who deserved to die.
He gave Philip
his crown, his robe,
and his signet ring,
and gave him instructions
to kill Lysias
and raise young Antiochus,
preparing him to be king
and to rule over the kingdom.

Then, in Persia, in the 149th year
of the Kingdom of the Greeks,   [163 B.C.E.]
Antiochus Epiphanes died.
"God Manifest to Men" was a corpse.
The "Light of the World" went out.

219

BALLAD 11
ANTIOCHUS EUPATOR

The New King

As soon as Lysias heard
that the king was dead,
he placed the crown
on the head of Antiochus,
the king's young son.

And he named the new king
Antiochus Eupator—
Antiochus "Son of a Noble Father."

Lysias had raised the young king
from the time when Antiochus Epiphanes
went off to Persia
in quest of fortune and glory.

Maccabee Attacks the Citadel

After the coronation,
a group of converted Jews,
looking for ways

to harm Judah Maccabee
and his brothers,
commandeered the Citadel.
Maccabee was determined
to destroy them.

In the 150th year
of the Kingdom of the Greeks,   [162 B.C.E.]
Maccabee and his men
besieged the Citadel
with catapults for tossing giant shot
and other engines of war.

After Judah's attack,
the troops in the Citadel fled
and joined other converts
living in Jerusalem.
A contingent went to Antioch
to see the young king,
Antiochus Eupator, and said,

"How long, my lord,
before you avenge us—
we who are as devoted to you
as we were
to your illustrious father,
whose decrees we always obeyed?

"The Jews who continue
to keep the law
despise us
for our loyalty to you

and our devotion
to Zeus the Father
and Dionysus his son.
It is they who are besieging
the Citadel.

"As soon as they capture
one of us, they kill him
and steal his possessions.

"They come not only against us
who dwell in the Citadel,
but against anyone like us
throughout Judea.

"If you do not stop them now,
you will never be able to stop them,
and they will do
a great deal more harm than this
to the king."

This incited young Antiochus.
He gathered about him
his advisors and friends,
officers in the infantry and cavalry,
and bands of mercenaries
from other kingdoms
and the Islands of the Sea.

They decided to raise a great army—
one hundred thousand infantry,
twenty thousand cavalry,
and thirty-two elephants

trained for war.
They were determined
to invade Judea
and lay siege to Jerusalem.

The Parade of the Mighty Army

The enemy army marched
through the region of Idumea,
and down the road
that leads to the city of Beth Zechariah,
not far from Jerusalem.
That evening they pitched camp.

The king rose early the next morning.
His army was ready for battle.
The trumpets sounded.
Young as he was,
Antiochus Eupator
marched in fierce determination
down the road
toward Beth Zechariah.

When Judah Maccabee received news
that the young king
was on the march
with a mighty army,
Maccabee ceased attacking the Citadel.
He turned his attention
to defeating the king,

and went forth from Jerusalem
toward Beth Zechariah.

The enemy assigned one elephant
to every few thousand foot soldiers,
each of whom wore
a coat of mail and a helmet
and carried a shield of polished brass
that gleamed like gold.
The enemy also assigned one elephant
to every few thousand cavalry,
the finest horsemen.

The Indian elephant trainers
were prepared for all eventualities.
Wherever the elephants were,
their trainers were there,
never departing from the sides
of the great animals.

On every elephant's back
was a war-howdah,
a well-made portable fort
constructed of wood
and held fast to the animal
by a cleverly designed harness.

Each howdah
held several warriors,
all buckled fast within,
who fought from the animal's back
while the trainer walked alongside.

Some of the cavalry walked or trotted
on both flanks of the army,
while others were scattered
within the ranks.

The sun striking the shields of brass
made the mountains glitter.

Half the king's army marched
high on the mountain,
the other half in the valley below.
Then the army on the ridge
began to descend.
When both halves merged,
they became one,
marching in single file,
orderly,
steadily,
inevitably.

Everyone who heard the noise
of that multitude,
and saw the marching
of that great army,
and saw the flashing
of the shining brass,
and heard the rattling
of all that armor
and the creaking
of all those harnesses
was stirred and filled with awe.

Maccabee and his men
drew near and watched
in fear and amazement
the mighty military parade.

Then Maccabee went forth
to engage the enemy in battle.

At once,
six hundred of the king's men fell.

Suddenly Eleazar Avaran,
Judah Maccabee's brother,
noticed that one of the elephants
stood out from all the others—
it was larger and taller
and was decorated
with the king's colors.
He was certain that the king himself
was riding on that elephant.

Eleazar Avaran was willing
to place himself in danger,
to sacrifice himself if necessary,
in order to save his people
and win glory for himself
and gain an everlasting name.

So he ran toward that elephant
with great courage.
Through the midst
of the raging conflict he ran,
slaying soldiers right and left,

clearing a path for himself
as he rushed rapidly onward
all the way to the beast!

On reaching his destination,
Eleazar Avaran
ducked under the elephant,
thrust his sword upward
into the monster's belly,
and killed it.
The elephant came falling down
on Eleazar,
instantly crushing
and killing him.

That charge was all in vain.
It did not kill the king,
nor did it make it possible
for others to capture him.

The Jews were horrified
by Eleazar's desperate act
and miserable death.
Seeing everywhere
the great power
of the king's forces
and the great potential
for violence,
the Jews were terrified.
Maccabee sounded the retreat,
and the Jews fled.

The field now empty of Jews,
the king's army resumed its march,
and went up to Jerusalem
to conquer it.

The King Marches on Jerusalem

Antiochus Eupator
pitched camp on Mount Zion,
near the Temple Mount.

Then he besieged
the Mount and the Temple,
placing artillery around the walls below
as well as engines of war—
catapults for casting fire and rock,
ballistas for shooting arrows,
and slings for hurling stones.
But the few Jews defending the Temple
held out.

As the battle raged,
the food supplies were running low.
It was a sabbatical year,
and the refugees
who had fled persecution
in the lands of the gentiles
were living on the last of the stores.
Only a few Jews remained
on the Temple Mount
because of the famine.

But the enemy soldiers below
were also running out of food.

The King Changes His Mind

Lysias now heard for the first time
that Antiochus Epiphanes,
just before he died,
had appointed Philip regent
to raise his son, young Antiochus.
This was startling news
because Antiochus Epiphanes,
just before leaving Antioch
in search of glory and treasure,
had appointed Lysias regent,
to raise the young boy to be king.

Philip, on leaving Persia,
returned to Syria
with Epiphanes' army.
It was Philip's intention
to usurp the rule
of the young and rightful king.

Lysias understood Philip's intentions.
He ran quickly to the king
to tell the news of Philip
and decide what should be done.

Lysias said, "Day by day
we waste away
from starvation,
and the place
we're trying to take
is strong,
and the Jews
are holding out.

"Let us reconcile with the Jews,
become their friends and allies,
and make peace with them
and their nation.

"Moreover,
let us make a treaty with them
that they may live
according to their religious laws,
as they did in former days.
They have fought us
simply because they are displeased
that we have abolished their religion.

"With the Jews on our side,
we won't have to worry
about Philip."

The king and his lords
were pleased with this advice.
So Eupator sent word
to Maccabee and his brothers
and all the people of Israel
that it was time for both sides

to make peace,
and to this end
Israel should send representatives
to Mount Zion,
to the king's headquarters.

The representatives of the Jews
came at once.
The young king
extended his right arm,
greeted them warmly, and said,

"Now that my father
has gone to the gods,
it is my sincerest wish
that all subjects of his kingdom
go about their business
with complete freedom of religion.

"I know that the Jews
did not agree
with my father's policy
of forcing them to adopt
the Greek religion and practices,
but preferred their own way of living
and asked only permission
to follow their own customs.

"I, too, only wish
that the nation of the Jews
live undisturbed and in peace,
that their Temple

be returned to them,
and that they follow
their ancestral customs.
Take comfort!
Be of good cheer!
For it shall be so!"

The representatives rejoiced.
Then Lysias and Eupator
took an oath before everyone
to remain friends of the Jews
forever!
To seal the oath,
Lysias and the king promised
that the soldiers in the Citadel of Jerusalem
would immediately evacuate.

Then Lysias and the king
marched from Mount Zion
into Jerusalem.
The moment they saw
its strength and splendor,
they instantly broke the oath
they'd so recently sworn,
and gave orders that the walls
around the Temple
be torn down,
reduced to rubble.
"Antiochus Eupator, the king,"
said Lysias,
"will fight Philip alone.
He has no need
of help from the Jews."

Then Eupator and Lysias
departed in haste for Antioch,
for they had heard
that Philip, the usurper,
was now ruling from there.

Eupator and Lysias
attacked Antioch,
captured the city,
killed Philip the usurper,
and boasted,
"We have done these things
without any help from the Jews."

Thereupon,
to the king's surprise,
his lords and army
deserted him—defected!—
and joined Philip's army.
Then they captured Lysias
and the king, too!

BALLAD 12
DEMETRIUS I

The Death of Antiochus Eupator

In the 151st year
of the Kingdom of the Greeks,
Demetrius I,
a nephew of Antiochus Epiphanes
and a cousin of Antiochus Eupator,
while held hostage in Rome,
escaped with the help of friends
and sailed to Syria,
to Seleucia-by-the-Sea,
the port city of Antioch,
the seat of his kingdom.

No sooner did Demetrius
enter the palace of his ancestors
and place the crown upon his head,
than he learned that his cousin
Antiochus Eupator
and Eupator's advisor, Lysias,
had killed Philip
and captured Antioch.
But the Syrian army
had captured Eupator and Lysias

and brought them to Demetrius's palace,
where they were right now!
The army awaited Demetrius's instructions.
Demetrius said,
"I cannot bear the sight of them!"

The soldiers, understanding him,
killed them both,
Antiochus Eupator and Lysias.
So Demetrius sat unopposed
on the throne of the kingdom.

News of Eupator's death
spread far and wide
throughout the Kingdom of the Greeks.
When it reached Athens,
Alexander,
the elder son of Antiochus Epiphanes
and older brother of Antiochus Eupator,
was surprised by the news.

Alexander
had relinquished
all claims to the throne,
choosing instead
to stay in Athens
and become a philosopher.

Now Alexander
changed his plans.
He would become a king
and a warrior—an educated one

like Alexander the Great,
for whom he was named—
and he would unseat Demetrius
and assume the throne.

Alcimus, the "High Priest"

At this time
some converted Jews
came to seek an audience
with Demetrius, the new king.
Their leader was a man named Alcimus,
whose chief ambition—
in spite of his love of Zeus—
was to become high priest of the Jews.

These men came before the king,
saying,

"Judah Maccabee and his brothers
not only have slain your friends
but have driven us out of our land.

"We implore you to punish Maccabee
and his brothers
and all who helped them."

So King Demetrius
appointed as general of his army
his dear friend Bacchides.

Demetrius also appointed Alcimus
as high priest of the Jews.
And he ordered the new high priest
to accompany Bacchides
with a great army
to take vengeance
on the children of Israel.

Bacchides and Alcimus
went into the land of Judea.
They sent envoys
to Maccabee and his brothers,
and deceitfully spoke of peace.

But Maccabee and his brothers
paid no heed,
for they could see
the great army of mighty warriors
nearby.

Now a delegation of scribes,
without Maccabee's knowledge,
took it upon themselves
to appear before Alcimus and Bacchides
for the purpose of obtaining
a just and peaceful solution.
These men were called Hasids—
religious, peace-loving, trusting,
and incapable of imagining
that anyone speaking of peace
would do them any harm.

The Hasids were certain
that Alcimus
was honorable and sincere.
They reasoned as follows,
"Alcimus is one of our own.
He is a priest of the line of Aaron,
a scholar of Torah,
even though he is a general
of the gentile army.
Surely no priest
would ever harm
his own people."

So they met with Alcimus,
who continued to speak of peace,
saying,
"We will not harm you
or your friends.
We only want peace."
And the Hasids believed him.

Then Alcimus said,
"To finalize our agreement,
I need to speak privately
with a contingent of your best men."
The Hasids agreed,
and Alcimus selected
sixty of their finest.
Accompanied by half his army,
Alcimus took the sixty men
to a secluded place,
where he slaughtered them.

Then he wrote down these words
from a psalm of David
and sent them mockingly
to the waiting Hasids:

"O Holy One, imagine!
The gentiles have come
into your inheritance.
They have defiled your holy Temple.
They have laid Jerusalem in ruins.
They have given the corpses
of your servants
to the birds of the sky for food,
and the flesh of your saints
to the beasts of the earth.
They have poured out their blood
like water
round about Jerusalem,
and there was none to bury them."

When the Hasids
who were waiting
for their sixty brothers
read the letter from the "high priest,"
they knew their companions
had been murdered.
Overcome with grief
and fear
and dread,
they said,
"There is neither truth
nor righteousness in these men,

for they have broken the agreement
and the oath they have sworn."

Thereupon Bacchides,
who was standing nearby
with the remaining army, said,
"You are quite right!"
and he massacred them, too.
It was an easy thing to do.

Then Bacchides
marched toward Jerusalem
and pitched his tents in Bethsaida.

After rounding up those of his men
who had opposed him—
gentile soldiers
who had not wanted
to murder innocent Jews—
Bacchides slaughtered them
and tossed them into a pit.

Then Bacchides placed Alcimus
in charge of Judea,
and returned to Antioch.

Alcimus was now surrounded
only with men who wanted
to destroy the children of Israel,
and being the sole commander
of the gentile army
and also the "high priest" of the Jews,
he was in a position

to inflict great harm
on the children of Israel.

When Judah Maccabee
saw all the evil that Alcimus
had already done,
he realized all the harm
he could yet do—
for some converts did evil
to the children of Israel
surpassing that
done by the gentiles.

Realizing this,
Maccabee went out
and round about
through the land of Judea,
all the way to its borders,
to take vengeance on those
who persecuted their fellow Jews.
And these tormentors were afraid
to set foot outside their homes.

Demetrius Sends Nicanor to Destroy Jerusalem

When Alcimus saw
Maccabee and his men—
how many they were
and how powerful—
he knew he could not prevail

against them.
So he returned to Antioch,
to Demetrius the king,
and reported all he had seen.

The king listened attentively.
This time he sent Nicanor,
one of his most honored generals—
a man who hated Jews
even more than Bacchides did—
with orders to destroy
the children of Israel.

Nicanor approached Jerusalem
with a mighty army,
which he left below the city.
With only a few troops,
he entered Jerusalem
speaking words of peace
and requesting a meeting
with Judah Maccabee.
Nicanor's real intent was to learn
the strength of Jerusalem.
Maccabee knew
Nicanor was treacherous,
and refused to meet with him.

Nicanor Visits the Temple

Nicanor went up to the Temple Mount.
Some of the priests

came out of the sanctuary
to greet him,
for the priests wanted peace
and were hoping
Nicanor wanted that, too.
They showed him
the burnt sacrifice they had offered
to honor Demetrius the king.

Nicanor extended his right arm,
feigning friendship,
but suddenly
he could not constrain himself,
and his true feelings came out.
He proceeded to taunt
and mock the priests,
to verbally abuse them
most shamefully,
and speak arrogantly to them.

"You are the priests of Israel,
the guardians of the law!
Law.
Superstitious nonsense!
Countless foolish rules
on how to serve an invisible—
nonexistent!—
god.

"In the temples of the Greeks
are beautiful statues,
images of the gods in heaven,

real gods, true gods,
because we can see them!

"We can light lamps to them
and burn incense to them, too.
We can pray to them.
We can touch them.
Why, we can even kiss them!
What can you do
to your invisible god?
Fools!
Blind fools!
You worship *nothing*!"

Then he threatened them.
"Unless you hand Maccabee
over to me,
I will return another time
with an army larger than this
and burn your Temple to the ground!"
And he turned his back on them
and departed in a rage,
shouting, "Brood of vipers
who claim to be
'sons of God'!"

The priests entered the Temple
and stood before the altar
weeping and praying,
"Almighty God,
you chose this House as your own,
to be a House of prayer,
a place for your people Israel

and for righteous gentiles, too—
a place to pray and cry for help.

"Take vengeance on this evil man.
Do not forget his wicked words.
Let them not come to fulfillment."

Maccabee Defeats Nicanor

When Nicanor left Jerusalem,
he realized that the city
might be too strong
even for his great army.
So he decided to engage Maccabee
down upon the plain.
He took his army
and they pitched their tents in Beth-Horon.

Maccabee made camp in Adasa
with three thousand men.
There he prayed, saying,
"Almighty Creator,
when the king of the Assyrians
sent men who spoke wicked words
against you,
your angel went forth and smote
five thousand of them and more.
Now likewise
destroy this host before us,
that others may know

their general has spoken
against you and your House."

It was on the thirteenth day
in the month of Adar
that the two armies joined in battle.

Nicanor was the first one killed,
and his army became frightened.
When the Syrians saw their general dead,
they cast down their arms and fled.

Maccabee pursued them
a full day's journey,
from Adasa all the way to Gezer,
shouting along the way
"Tuh ROO ah"—
the command for the trumpets
to sound the alarm.
The trumpets blared,
"RA ta ta, RA ta ta, RA ta ta, TAA."

On hearing that sound,
young Jewish men
came running forth from every direction
from all the surrounding towns
of Judea
and hemmed the enemy in.

The enemy turned
to face their pursuers
and were slain by the sword.
Not one man lived.

Then Maccabee hacked off
Nicanor's head and hand—
the right hand he used so mockingly—
and he placed them on poles
carried at the front of his army.
On reaching Jerusalem,
he hung the head and hand on high.

The people rejoiced greatly,
for the men of Judea
had won a great victory.

BALLAD 13
THE ROMANS

The Fame of the Romans

Judah Maccabee heard
of the fame of the Romans.
How mighty and powerful they were!
They accepted in friendship
any nation allying itself with them.
Oh, how mighty they were,
and how powerful!

He learned
of their noble wars
and the heroic things they did
on behalf of those they conquered.
Consider the Galatians.
After the Romans defeated them,
they gave them the privilege
of paying tribute to Rome!

And look at all the Romans did
for the Spanish!
After taking over
the silver and gold mines in Spain,
they took over the entire country!

Judah learned
how the Romans
went to the ends of the earth
to fight kings,
and how they crushed every one
who rose up against them,
and then,
in their generosity,
permitted those kings
to pay taxes to Rome every year!

Judah Maccabee heard
how Antiochus "the Great,"
the father of Antiochus Epiphanes,
had marched against Rome
with one hundred twenty elephants,
with cavalry and chariots,
and a very great infantry.
But the Romans defeated him,
took him alive,
kept him hostage,
and took away from him
the beautiful lands
of India, Media, and Lydia.

Then, in their merciful goodness,
on realizing how truly weak he was,
the Romans let Antiochus "the Great" go,
and made covenants with him
and let him
pay great tribute to Rome.

Judah Maccabee learned
how the king of Macedonia
and the kings of the city-states of Greece
had decided to make war on Rome and destroy it.
But the Romans sent an army,
conquered them all,
slaughtered many Greek men,
carried away the choicest
along with the women and children,
and took the spoils.
Then Rome took over these places
and reduced the survivors to slavery,
a state in which she kept them still!

Judah learned
how the Romans had crushed
and brought under their rule
every kingdom and island
that showed any resistance to them.

But with their allies—
and all who put their trust in them—
the Romans were true friends
and could be relied upon!

Those to whom Rome
chose to give a kingdom
still reigned as kings,
while those from whom Rome
chose to take away a kingdom
had disappeared
from the face of the earth!

And yet,
as much as the Romans
loved to have kings
ruling over the lands
that they conquered,
the Romans since ancient days
had never had a king
rule over them.
For the people of Rome
did not trust kings
to rule them,
but only to rule others.

As for themselves,
the Romans had created the Senate,
a body of noble men
who sat in session every day,
always deliberating
for the good of the people
and serving them well.

The Romans had placed
at the head of their government
a consul—
one man,
serving for one year.
All others were obedient to him.
And there was no envy or jealousy,
for such feelings did not exist
among the Romans.

Maccabee's Alliance with Rome

Judah Maccabee listened
and considered these things.
Then he chose Jason ben Eleazar
and Eupolemus, son of John ben Hakkoz,
and sent them to Rome
to make an alliance of friendship,
and to entreat the Romans
to lift the Greek yoke from them.
For the Kingdom of the Greeks
had all but enslaved Israel.

Eupolemus and Jason went to Rome,
a very long journey from Judea,
and they entered the Senate and said,

"Judah Maccabee and his brothers
and the Jewish people have sent us
to make a peace agreement with you,
and to be written among your allies
and your friends."

Well, the men of the Senate
sat up in their seats,
for that pleased them greatly—
a peace agreement between great Rome
and tiny Judea!

And the Senate responded
in a letter written on tablets of brass
to be sent to Jerusalem and hung there
as a permanent memorial

252

of the covenant of peace
and the alliance
between Rome and Jerusalem.
And this is what the tablets said:

> Great good upon the Romans
> and the Jewish people
> by sea and by land forever!
> May the enemy's sword
> be ever far from them!
>
> But if war should come to the Romans
> or anywhere in the Roman Empire,
> the Jewish people shall help them
> with all their heart at their time of need
> whenever they are called upon.
> They shall not give anything
> to those who make war on Rome—
> no aid, no food,
> no arms, no money,
> no ships, nor anything else
> the Romans consider of value.
> And they shall keep this covenant
> without recompense.
>
> Likewise, if war should come
> to the Jewish nation,
> the Romans shall help them
> with all their heart at their time of need
> whenever they are called upon.
> The Romans shall not give food
> to any who make war on the Jews,

no arms, no money,
no ships, nor anything else
the Romans consider of value.
And they shall keep this covenant
without deceit.

By these articles do the Romans
make a covenant
with the Jewish people.

Now should it happen at a later date
that one party or the other
thinks it appropriate to add or subtract
anything stated here,
they may do so as they wish.
And whatever it is they add or take away
shall be ratified.

In addition to the letter on tablets of brass,
the Romans wrote this letter on parchment:

As for the evils King Demetrius
has done to the Jews,
we have written to him as follows:

Why have you placed a heavy yoke
upon our friends and allies the Jews?
If you do one more thing
to give them cause for complaint,
we will declare war on you and fight you
by land and by sea,
and we will make sure
that the Jews receive justice.

King Demetrius received this letter
at the same time he learned
that Nicanor and the Syrian army
had fallen in battle.
Thereupon, Demetrius sent Bacchides
and Alcimus with a great army
to invade the land of Judea
a second time.

They marched down the Gilgal road,
and pitched their tents
before the ascent to Arbela,
a great city in Galilee,
and attacked and conquered it,
slaying many.
So much did Demetrius
honor and respect
the letter from Rome!

As for Rome,
why should she honor
an alliance with Judea
and send Roman legions
all that distance
by land or by sea
just to defend or avenge
the Jews?

For all Rome knew
that the Jews were a people
who had made no contribution

to civilization
and whose only pleasures were
to worship
an invisible god,
to cherish
a nonsensical book of rules,
and to plow
a worthless,
uninhabitable,
and minuscule
piece of land
they called a country.

BALLAD 14
"HOW ARE THE MIGHTY FALLEN"

The Incident at Jaffa

Shortly after Maccabee's victory
over Nicanor,
the gentiles of Jaffa
committed an outrageous crime.

They expelled the Jews of Jaffa,
making them embark on boats
docked in the harbor.
When the Jews put out to sea,
their boats overloaded
with people and baggage,
the gentiles pursued
in swift and unencumbered boats,
overtook them,
swamped the boats,
and sank them,
drowning all the passengers.

When Judah Maccabee
heard of this barbarity,
he came by night to Jaffa,
set fire to the docks,

set fire to the ships,
and killed the people.

The light from that blaze
could be seen
all the way to Jerusalem.

Maccabee's Last Battle

During the first month
of the 152nd year
of the Kingdom of the Greeks,   [160 B.C.E.]
Bacchides encamped in the plain
below Jerusalem
and marched toward Beeroth
with twenty thousand infantry
and two thousand cavalry.

Judah Maccabee
pitched his tents at Elasa
with three thousand
of his best men.
On seeing the multitude
and might of the enemy,
Maccabee's men became terrified
and most of them deserted.
Of three thousand,
at most eight hundred remained.

Judah Maccabee
was greatly troubled

by the cowardice of his men.
After all, the Jews
had been outnumbered before.

Moreover,
there was no time now
to gather reinforcements
and no town nearby
from which to get them.
Maccabee said to his brave remnant,
outnumbered by more than
twenty-five to one,
"Men of Israel!
We can still put up a fight!"

But his men were discouraged and said,
"Judah, we can't fight them
when we are so greatly outnumbered.
Let us run for our lives
and get reinforcements.
Then we can return and fight."

Judah Maccabee replied,
"There's no place to run,
no place to hide,
no reinforcements to be had.
We have no choice but to fight.
If our time has come,
at least let us die like men,
defending our people,
our religion,
and our country.

"We can never conform
to the ways of the gentiles,
to the ways of those
who arrogantly proclaim
that they alone hold the truth.
We can never stain our honor
by giving in to such a terrible lie.

"My brave men of Israel,
we must stand our ground.
We cannot disgrace
all that we have accomplished,
and all that remains to be done."

While Maccabee was speaking,
Bacchides' soldiers
were coming out of their tents
and standing about,
looking at Judah's men,
sizing them up.

Bacchides' cavalry split into two divisions
and flanked the mass of infantry,
which then divided in two.
The stone-slingers and archers were out front
along with a strong company
of foot soldiers.

The two flanks of cavalry advanced,
sounding trumpets.
Bacchides was in the right flank.

Judah Maccabee's men
had no prescribed formation,
but adapted and moved in response
to each new situation.

Maccabee shouted,
"Men of Israel,
courage!
Be strong!
Fear not!
My valiant men of Israel,
to battle!"

The earth shook
at the tramp and sound
of the marching armies.
Trumpets on both sides
sounded the charge.
Men on both sides
raised battle cries.
And the battle began.
It raged from morning till evening.

When Maccabee saw
that the right flank—
the one under Bacchides' command—
had most of the might,
he took his best men to attack it.
They fell upon the enemy
and broke and scattered
their solid ranks

like a gust of wind
scatters a pile of leaves.
Then, thrusting themselves
through the midst of the enemy,
they killed most of them
and chased the rest
to the mountain slopes.

Judah, turning toward heaven,
shouted, "Maccabee!"

His men shouted
over and over again,
"Maccabee!
Maccabee!
Maccabee!"

When the left flank saw
that the right was defeated and in retreat,
it turned and chased
Judah Maccabee and his men,
and soon was nipping at their heels.

Maccabee and his men
were completely surrounded.
The situation was desperate.
Unable to flee,
they turned to face the enemy.

One of Maccabee's men
prayed softly, "Hosanna!"

A great conflict ensued,
and many men on both sides
were wounded and killed.
Judah Maccabee himself fell,
and his men fled.

The enemy captain of the left flank
walked up to the body,
lifted the helmet, and set it aside.
The face of the dead man
was unmistakable—
the distinct and noble features.

The captain thought,
"How curious
that the fiercest of warriors
has such a beautiful face."
He did not even notice that the face
was weather-beaten and scarred.

Then he clasped Judah's right arm
in his own and noticed the hand.
He inspected the other and thought,
"Never have I seen
more magnificent hands."

He removed his own helmet,
cradled it in his arm,
and said to his troops,
"Men, today we have won a great victory.
For the man lying before you
is Judah Maccabee,

the greatest leader of our age
and one of the greatest commanders
of all time."
Then he added,
"Too bad he was a Jew!"

Then the captain and his troops
joined Bacchides and his men
on the mountain slope.

For a while,
the enemy gazed
at the body in the field,
as graceful in death
as it had been in life.
Finally they departed into the hills.

Judah Maccabee's Funeral

Jonathan and Simon lifted up
the body of their brother Judah,
the one called Maccabee.
His men,
even those who had deserted him,
marched behind.
They carried him to the town of Modin,
where they buried him
in the tomb of his ancestors.

The people wailed
and through their sobbing
said words of David:

"Your beauty, O Israel,
upon your high places is slain!
How are the mighty fallen!"

"How are the mighty fallen
in the midst of the battle!"

The men who had fought
at Judah's side
and the deserters, too,
stood and wept
along with his brothers.
At first one or two murmured,
"Maccabee!"

The murmuring spread
and became a chant,
"Maccabee!
Maccabee!
Maccabee!"

It grew louder
and louder
and louder
until it was so thunderous
it reached to heaven
and the ends of the earth.

Then came a silence
louder than the shouting,
followed by the call
of the trumpet,
"Ta RA, ta RA, ta RAA."

All Israel lamented Maccabee greatly
and mourned for many days,
saying,
"How are the mighty fallen,
saving Israel."

BALLAD 15
JONATHAN ABBA

Jonathan Becomes Commander in Chief

After Judah Maccabee died,
the Jews who had forsaken the Creator
and the ways of their ancestors
and had adopted the religion of the Greeks
once again
began to show their faces in public
in all the coastal towns of Israel.
There were many such men,
and they did much harm.

In those days, too,
there was a great famine,
and many faithful Jews
were dying of starvation.
Their converted brothers
promised to feed them,
if only they'd convert.

Conditional love is counterfeit,
but starving men succumb to hunger,
not to the quality of love.

Bacchides appointed
the most zealous of the converts
as governors throughout Judea.
These governors made inquiries
about Maccabee's friends
and searched them out.

Whenever they found them,
they seized them
and brought them before Bacchides,
who humiliated them,
insulted them,
and called them names—
 "Serpents!" "Vipers!" and the like.
Bacchides spat upon them,
struck them, beat them,
and tortured them.
And then he killed them.
There was great affliction in Israel.

Maccabee's friends gathered
and went to Jonathan, his brother,
and said,
"Ever since Judah Maccabee died,
we've had no one
to fight the enemies of our nation.
We want you,
Jonathan Apphus—Abba!—
to be our leader,
our commander in chief,
to take Maccabee's place
and fight for freedom
and fight for us."

Jonathan Apphus,
son of Mattathias, accepted
and took his brother's place,
his brother Judah Maccabee.

When Bacchides heard this,
he was determined to kill Jonathan
and his brother Simon
and all those with them.
On learning Bacchides' intentions,
Jonathan and Simon fled
into the wilderness of Tekoa—
Tekoa, the hometown
of the prophet Amos,
the prophet who preached,
"Let justice roll down like waters,
and righteousness
like an ever-flowing stream."

Jonathan and Simon pitched their tents
in the wilderness of Tekoa
by the waters of the Asphar pool.
When Bacchides heard this,
he ordered his army
to cross the Jordan
in search of Jonathan
on a Sabbath day.

The Death of John Gaddi

John Gaddi, eldest son of Mattathias,
was a leader of the multitudes.
He organized many projects—
raising funds to help the poor,
providing services and care
for the infirm,
finding every orphan a home.

Jonathan Apphus sent John Gaddi,
his eldest brother,
to entreat some Nabateans,
Arabs on the side of the Jews,
to hold in safekeeping
Jonathan's and Simon's
excess flocks and herds,
because tending too many animals
was an encumbrance
while waging war.

John Gaddi encountered the Arabs
outside the city of Madaba.
They agreed to guard the animals.
Just then a crowd of people
all dressed up for a wedding,
but concealing daggers
beneath their finery,
came forth from Madaba.
It was the wealthy family
of the bridegroom,
with their friends and guests.

On seeing all that livestock
with so few men to guard it,
they fell upon
John Gaddi and the Arabs
and massacred them.
They took the animals
and went on their way.

The family of the bride
came from the city of Nadabath
with a great retinue,
for she was the daughter
of a great lord of Canaan.

Jonathan and Simon,
upon learning of the massacre
of their brother,
were determined to take revenge.
They went up into the mountains
just below the pass
between Nadabath and Madaba,
and hid and waited.

Soon they heard a loud commotion
just above them.
Simon and Jonathan looked up
and saw a great crowd of people,
all dressed up for a wedding
but tending flocks and herds!

The bridegroom,
surrounded by family and friends,

came forth to meet the bridal party.
All began to dance and sing
while musicians played flutes
and stringed instruments
and banged on drums.

In the middle of the revelry,
Jonathan and his men
ambushed them,
killing many.
The survivors fled
into the mountains.

Thus did Jonathan avenge
the murder of his brother.
And he took back his animals
and took as spoils
the wedding gifts.

Then Jonathan and Simon
wept for their brother John,
who had loved peace, hated war,
and done so many deeds
in the service of those
who had no one else to help them.

And through their tears they said,
"For the good hand of God
was on him."

Then they turned their attention
to the river Jordan,
where Bacchides was camped.

The Battle at the Jordan

Bacchides and his mighty army
were waiting near the marsh
by the banks of the Jordan
on that Sabbath day
when skies were gray
and rumbling.

On seeing the enemy,
Jonathan said to his men,
"Let us attack at once,
for we have no other choice.
Before us is the enemy,
behind us is the river,
on either sides
are marsh and wood.
There's no place to retreat."

One of his brave young men
began to pray loudly
in the words of the prophet,
"Righteous are you, O YHV,
whenever I complain to you.
Well, I have a complaint
for you right now.
Why do the wicked prosper?
Why do the treacherous thrive?
You plant them and they take root;
they grow and bear fruit."

He concluded his prayer
with these words of his own:
"I love you, O God,
but I do not understand this.
Please explain it to me!"

Jonathan nodded and smiled,
but Bacchides,
on overhearing this prayer,
said, "How strange are the Jews!
How strange are their prayers!"
Then the two armies engaged in battle.

Suddenly a thunderstorm struck.
Lightning was flashing
and crashing to the ground.
Thunder boomed and roared.
Rain came down in sheets so dark
it was hard to see the warriors.
Jonathan came upon Bacchides
altogether by chance.
He was just about to kill him
when Bacchides disappeared
in the downpour.

Jonathan and many of his men
jumped into the Jordan
and waded or swam
to the opposite shore.

When the sun came out,
many dead bodies from both sides
were floating in the marsh,

but not a corpse or a living man
was to be seen on high ground.
For Bacchides had retreated
to Jerusalem,
and Jonathan had fled to Tekoa.

The Death of Alcimus

Alcimus,
the "high priest" of the Jews—
the priest who worshiped
Dionysus, the son,
and Zeus, the Father—
was about to give orders
to tear down
the walls of the inner courtyard
of the Temple
and to toss the books of the Prophets
into the fire.
But at that very moment,
during the 153rd year
of the Kingdom of the Greeks,
in the second month,
on the seventh day,
his plans came to a halt,
for Alcimus suffered a stroke.

All at once
he could not move his limbs,
and he could not utter a word,

let alone give orders
regarding the Temple.
After sustaining a series of seizures
in swift succession,
Alcimus suddenly sighed,
and then he died.

A Moment of Peace

Bacchides,
who witnessed Alcimus's strange death,
went to Demetrius to report it.
The king was terrified,
for he was sure it was an omen.

As a result,
the entire land of Judea
was left in peace for two whole years,
and the Jews were happy—
plowing, planting, and harvesting.

But there were men
who could not bear to see
the children of Israel
enjoying a moment of peace.

Converts despised Sabbath joys
and Sabbath peace—
they hated peace of any sort.
So they came together
to take counsel, saying,

"Look how Jonathan enjoys life!
He spends his days with his wife,
playing or working with his children,
cultivating the land,
and sitting without fear
'under his vine and under his fig tree.'

"Why don't we bring Bacchides here
to change all that?
In one night he could kill them all."

So they went to talk to Bacchides,
who immediately
raised a great army
to carry out their wishes.

The Defeat of Bacchides

Jonathan learned of Bacchides' plan.
He went with his brother Simon
to Beth Basi in the desert,
a walled city, well fortified,
a good place
from which to fight Bacchides.

Bacchides sent word
to his converted friends
throughout Judea to join him.
They laid siege to Beth Basi

with engines of war,
and the battle raged for many days,
but Jonathan defeated Bacchides
with great carnage of his army.
It was a great victory
for Jonathan.

Bacchides realized
that all the advice he'd received
and all the things he'd done
to wipe out the Jews
were in vain.

Why had he done it?
he asked himself repeatedly.
Why had Demetrius
ordered him to do it?
What had the Jews ever done
except wish to live in peace
and be given the right
to practice their own religion?

On realizing
all the lives lost for nothing,
Bacchides became enraged
at his Jewish advisors,
all converts to the Greek religion.

It was these men
who had advised him
to come to Judea
to oppress and persecute
the faithful children of Israel.

Their advice was his undoing.
So he rounded up these "friends"—
as many as he could—
and killed them.

Then he decided to go home,
to Antioch.

Jonathan and Bacchides Make Peace

When Jonathan learned
of Bacchides' intention
to leave Judea,
he sent emissaries
to make peace.
And he handed over
all prisoners of war.

Bacchides eagerly accepted
the terms of peace.
He released his Jewish prisoners
and swore he would come no more
to Judea,
and never again harm
the children of Israel.

Then Bacchides went home—
back to Syria—
and he kept his word.
He never again returned

to Judea,
and he never again harmed
the Jews.

Jonathan executed
the traitors of his people.
Then he went and dwelled
in the town of Michmash,
famous for its wheat
and delicious bread.
He ruled from there
and judged wisely.

And once more
the sword ceased from Israel.

BALLAD 16
ALEXANDER

Alexander Conquers Acre

It was in the 160th year
of the Kingdom of the Greeks   [152 B.C.E.]
that Alexander,
the elder son of Antiochus Epiphanes,
attacked and conquered
the city of Acre.
With great acclamation,
the people crowned him
as their king,
for the people loved him
as they had loved his younger brother,
Antiochus Eupator,
and they despised Demetrius.

Alexander's Youth

When Alexander was a boy,
his father, recognizing
his son's great intelligence,
had sent him away to school,

to Athens,
to the very Academy
that Plato, the famous philosopher,
had founded
just outside the city.

The Academy was untouched by war.
Even those who invaded Athens
always chose to spare it—
they revered it so.

Alexander loved Athens
and the Academy,
and wrote to his father
and told him so.
Alexander advised his father
to make Alexander's younger brother—
the boy who became
Antiochus Eupator—
the heir apparent,
for Alexander had no intention
of ever returning home,
of ever becoming king.

The students and teachers
at the Academy
had all been born into the Greek religion.
But by the time they left school,
many had come to doubt it.

Philosophy and rigorous thinking
had convinced them
that a belief or faith in the gods

was based on dogmatism,
a belief system
of absolute totalitarian authority—
arbitrary, devoid of reason,
and learned by rote.

In philosophical debate
and discussion,
dogmatism crumbled,
for it was indefensible
in the face of reason.

Shortly before Alexander
became a student,
the concept of probability
came into existence at the Academy.
Probability showed
that only agnosticism—
"I don't know"
where the existence
of the gods was concerned—
was rational and defensible.

Alexander saw
that probability could become
one of the greatest liberating forces
in human intellectual development
and a surprisingly practical
guide for living.

But few outside the Academy
had the courage to accept it.

They preferred to find meaning
where there was none,
in coincidence,
and preferred the certainty
that comes only with faith in the gods.

Alexander mused,
"Certainty is not possible.
And there is no foe
so deadly to the quest for truth
as the certainty that one possesses it.

"Well then,
how can anyone impose
his religious beliefs upon another?
My father has been wrong to do so."

Alexander was very different
from his father.

Demetrius Makes Jonathan an "Ally"

When Demetrius learned
of Alexander's conquest of Acre,
he called his advisors together
and said to them,
"Let us make peace with Jonathan
before Alexander does,
lest both of them join
to fight against us."

So Demetrius sent Jonathan a letter
with words of friendship,
filled with flattery and praise,
giving him authority
to raise an army
and requesting his alliance in war.

Demetrius also gave orders
that the children of Israel held hostage
by their converted brothers
in the Citadel in Jerusalem
be immediately released.

When the converts saw the orders,
they became alarmed
and were concerned
for their own safety.
Reluctantly, they obeyed,
releasing the hostages
and sending them home.

Then Jonathan decided
to build his home in Jerusalem
and settle there.

Alexander Appoints Jonathan High Priest

At the same time
that Demetrius was courting Jonathan,
Alexander learned of all the battles

Jonathan and his brothers had fought,
of all the noble deeds they had performed,
of all the pains they had endured
for the sake of religious freedom
and the liberty of their nation.

Alexander said to his aides,
"Where shall we find
another man like this?
Let us make Jonathan
our ally and friend."

So Alexander wrote Jonathan a letter saying,

> From King Alexander
> to Jonathan, his brother:
> Greetings!
>
> We have heard
> of your strength in war
> and want you to be our friend.
> Accordingly,
> on this very day,
> we appoint you high priest
> of your nation.
>
> We bestow upon you the honor
> of being called the king's friend.
>
> We are sending you
> a gold crown and a purple robe
> to signify these things.
> For your part, we request
> only your friendship.

It was in the seventh month
of the 160th year
of the Kingdom of the Greeks,   [152 B.C.E.]
during the festival of Sukkot,
that Jonathan Apphus
was dressed in priestly robes
and was ordained high priest of Israel.

The sukkah in the Temple courts
had been decorated with
"the fruit of the hadar tree,
branches of palm trees,
boughs of leafy trees,
and willows of the brook."

Jonathan had wished
a simple ceremony
to take place in the sukkah
with only his family,
the priests, and the elders attending.
But so many people had gathered
on the Temple Mount
and in the outer Temple court
to catch a glimpse
of the new high priest
that the priests and elders advised
that the ceremony be moved
from the sukkah
onto the landing
between the Temple courts.

When the people saw
the seat of the high priest being moved
from the sukkah to the landing,
their hearts leaped up.
And when they saw Jonathan
leave the sukkah,
the crowds went wild with cheering,
waving palm branches vigorously,
and shouting, "Abba! Abba! Abba!"
"Papa! Papa! Papa!"

Jonathan ascended the stairs
and took his seat.
A hush fell over the people.

As was the custom
at the ordination of the high priest
or the coronation of a king of Israel,
a priest anointed Jonathan
with the finest olive oil
and chanted these words of David:
"I will tell of the decree of YHV.
He said to me, 'You are my son;
today I have begotten you.'"

Then the priest chanted
words from the prophet:
"I will be his father,
and he shall be my son."

And Jonathan responded
by chanting this psalm:

"YHV is my shepherd.
I shall not want.
He makes me lie down in green pastures.
He leads me beside still waters.
He restores my soul.
He leads me in the paths of righteousness
for his name's sake.
Even though I walk
through the valley of the shadow of death,
I fear no evil,
for you are with me.
Your rod and your staff comfort me.
You prepare a table before me
in the presence of my enemies.
You anoint my head with oil.
My cup overflows.
Surely goodness and mercy
shall follow me
all the days of my life.
And I shall dwell in the House of YHV
forever."

Then Jonathan stood and,
raising his hands over the whole assembly,
gave them God's blessing:

"YHV bless you and keep you.
YHV make his face to shine upon you,
and be gracious to you.
YHV lift up his countenance upon you
and give you peace."

Then Jonathan departed.
As commander in chief
of all Judea,
he raised an army
equipped with many weapons.

Demetrius "Recognizes" the State of Judea

When Demetrius heard
what Alexander had done,
he was annoyed,
and he said to his men,

"How is it possible
that Alexander has become
a friend of the Jews
ahead of us,
thereby strengthening himself?

"I will write another letter
to the Jews
and promise them many things
and give them reason
to hope for them all.
And I will promise them
many other gifts besides,
just to win their support.
And first among them,
I shall recognize the Jewish nation."

So he sent a very long letter
filled with many promises,
addressed to the "Jewish nation":

> From King Demetrius
> to the Jewish nation:
> Greetings!
>
> Insofar as you have kept
> your treaties with us
> and continue to be our friends,
> not allying yourselves
> with our enemies—
> we have heard all this
> and are glad of it!—
> and if you continue to be loyal,
> we will pay you back
> by granting you special privileges
> and exemptions in abundance
> and other benefits besides.
>
> Here is what I am going to do for you:
> I release the Jews from tributes,
> from the salt tax,
> from the crown tax,
> and from all those things
> normally owed the king—
> namely, one-third of the seed,
> and one-half the produce
> of the fruit trees.
> I release you from these obligations
> from this day forth.
>
> And I am going to do even more:
> Let the holy city of Jerusalem

and the land round about it
be free from taxes and tributes.

As for the Citadel of Jerusalem,
I relinquish all authority over it,
which I transfer to the high priest,
and he may choose any men he likes
to guard it.

Moreover,
I am setting free
all Jewish prisoners of war
who have been carried away
from Judea as slaves
into all parts of my kingdom. . . .

Furthermore,
all Jewish holidays,
Sabbaths,
New Moon festivals,
and the High Holy Days—
and also three days before
and three days after
the holiday—
shall be days of no work
and freedom for all the Jews
in my kingdom.
And no one shall have
the authority to interfere
with the Jewish holidays
or to bother the Jews
in any way.

Moreover,
it is my will
that there shall be enlisted

BALLAD 16: ALEXANDER

in the king's army
thirty thousand Jews,
who shall be paid the same salaries
as the other soldiers of the king.
And Jews shall be placed
in the fortresses of the king,
while others shall be
set in charge of running
the affairs of the kingdom—
all trusted positions.

Furthermore,
it is my will that the Jews
living throughout my kingdom
outside of Judea
shall have Jewish governors,
and all the Jews shall live
in accordance
with their own religious laws.

Concerning
the three districts of Samaria,
let them be unified with Judea,
to be reckoned as one government,
and to be bound
by no other authority
than the high priest's.

As for the city of Acre
and its land,
I give it as a free gift
to the Temple at Jerusalem
to provide the necessary funds
for maintenance of the Temple.
Moreover,

every year I shall give
fifteen thousand shekels of silver
from the king's treasury,
and any surplus shall also be given,
toward the maintenance
of the Temple in Jerusalem.

Besides all this,
I shall give
five thousand shekels of silver,
the same amount taken
as the Temple dues each year.
That money shall be returned,
for it rightfully belongs
to the priests
who conduct worship there,
for it was always meant
for their salaries.

Whoever flees
to the Temple at Jerusalem
to seek sanctuary
because he is indebted to the king
or for any other reason
shall be forgiven his debts.

As for the maintenance
of the Temple,
funds shall come directly
from the king's accounts—
and this applies also
to the maintenance
of the walls of Jerusalem
and the walls throughout Judea.

When Jonathan and the Jewish people
heard Demetrius's promises,
they paid no heed
because they did not believe him.
What good were the promises of Demetrius?
The Jews well remembered
the terrible harm
he had done in Israel,
how greatly he had afflicted her.

But the terms proposed by Alexander
pleased the Jewish people greatly,
for Alexander, of all the gentile kings,
was the first to make
a sincere peace treaty with them,
and they were therefore determined
to be his ally forever.

Alexander Slays Demetrius and Becomes King of the East

Alexander raised a great army
to fight Demetrius.
Alexander attacked,
and Demetrius fled.
But Alexander gave chase
and forced Demetrius to fight.

The battle raged long and hard
from sunrise to sunset.

And before evening had come,
Alexander was victorious
and Demetrius was dead.

Alexander thereby became
the one and only
king of Syria
and all its provinces—
Alexander, king of the East.

Alexander's Marriage

Alexander sent ambassadors
to Ptolemy Philometor,
king of Egypt,
carrying this message:

> I have returned to my own country,
> where I sit upon the throne
> of my ancestors,
> for I have won back my kingdom
> by conquering Demetrius. . . .
>
> Therefore,
> let us make an alliance
> of friendship between us
> and let us seal it
> by making your daughter my wife.
> I shall be your son-in-law,
> and give you
> and your daughter

> gifts in accordance with
> the great honor
> you both deserve.

Ptolemy, king of Egypt,
responded, saying:

> Happy the day
> you returned to the land
> of your ancestors
> and sat on the throne
> of your kingdom!
>
> It gives me great joy
> to do as you requested.
> Let us meet at the city of Acre
> that we may come to know one another,
> and there I shall give you
> my daughter in marriage,
> just as you wish.

So in the 162nd year
of the Kingdom of the Greeks,
Ptolemy went out of Egypt
with his daughter,
and marched to the city of Acre,
and met Alexander there.

Ptolemy gave his daughter
in marriage to Alexander.
And the celebration took place
with great splendor.

Alexander had sent an invitation
to Jonathan Apphus,
asking him to attend his marriage.
Jonathan was honored to do so.
He went to Acre
and gave the two kings,
the bride,
and all members of the wedding party
many gifts of silver and gold.
And everyone liked Jonathan
because everyone always liked Jonathan.

Alexander Honors Jonathan

At that time
certain men of Israel,
converts to the Greek gods,
gathered together and conspired
to slander Jonathan.
They said he liked to sleep
with gentile women
and that he was plotting
to kill Alexander
and that he wanted
to conquer the world.

But Alexander would not listen.
Instead, he ordered Jonathan
to appear before him
in the presence of these men,

and he ordered them
to dress Jonathan
in robes of purple.

Then Alexander called together
all his lords and said to them,

"Take Jonathan
to the center of the city
and make this proclamation
before the people:

"No one
shall speak ill of Jonathan,
and no one
shall make trouble for him,
but everyone shall honor him."

When Jonathan's slanderers heard this,
they knew the words
were meant for them,
and when they saw
the honors heaped upon Jonathan
by the king,
they fled from the kingdom.

Alexander further honored Jonathan
by making him
one of his principal advisors
and one of his best friends.

Alexander
immediately invited Jonathan
to dine with him.
Jonathan accepted.

During a banquet of fish,
they discussed many subjects,
but particularly philosophy.
Then their discussion
turned to religion,
and Alexander asked,
"What is the essence
of the Jewish religion?"

"The essence of our religion
was best expressed
by one of our prophets, who said,
'It has been told you, O man,
what is good
and what YHV requires of you:
Only to do justly,
and to love kindness,
and to walk humbly
with your God.'"

"That is as beautiful
as it is excellent.
Can you reduce
the prophet's words
even more?"

"The Torah commands:
'Love your neighbor as yourself.'"

"Ah, my friend,
a noble commandment,
but impossible to fulfill;
for much evil is done
in the name of love.
Besides,
how many people
can love their neighbor?"

Both men laughed.

Jonathan said, "Perhaps that is why
God gave the commandment!"

They laughed again.

"Alexander, what is the essence
of the Greek religion?"

"Merely to believe in the gods,
to have faith in them.
I do not know if the gods exist,
but if they do,
I have no faith in them."

"But you
are a highly moral man."

"My friend,
never confuse morality with religion.
My father was

301

the most religious man
I've ever known,
but he had no morality at all.
And the Greek religion
is the most intolerant of religions,
as you well know.
And because intolerance is not concerned
with morality,
but only with faith in the gods,
it will threaten nonbelievers
with torture and even murder
to force them—
for their own good, of course—
to believe in the gods!"

"How, then,
does a Greek learn morality?
Through philosophy?"

"Only the philosophers
would say so."

Both men laughed again.

Alexander said, "Philosophy
is an intellectual exercise
and does not affect behavior.
But philosophy has shown
that dialogue can be
a powerful tool
for conceptualization
and clarification.
Dialogue may yet lead us

to discover this evening
the meaning of
'Love your neighbor.'"

Jonathan said,
"Authentic morality
requires action, not words.
It is learned
mainly by observing
examples of kindness
and abhorrence of cruelty
set by people
in their ordinary deeds."

"Jonathan, you are saying that
the commandment should be
'Be kind to your neighbor,'
not 'love' him."

"That is my interpretation
of the commandment.
And, if one cannot be kind,
then at least one should not be cruel.
Don't harm your neighbor."

"So the essence
of the commandment is
'Do no harm.'"

Jonathan replied, "Yes,
I think so."

And Alexander said, "I agree."

Dialogue and dinner over,
Jonathan retired.
The next morning after breakfast,
he thanked Alexander
for the many honors
Alexander had bestowed upon him,
for the generous hospitality
Alexander had lavished upon him,
and especially for their friendship,
which allowed them
to discuss honestly
ideas that affected not only them
but also Jews and gentiles
everywhere in the world.

Afterwards,
Jonathan returned to Jerusalem
safely and joyously.

Demetrius II Challenges Jonathan

In the 165th year
of the Kingdom of the Greeks,   [147 B.C.E.]
Demetrius II,
son of Demetrius I,
whom Alexander had slain,
sailed from Crete to Syria,
the land of his ancestors,
and declared himself king.

304

When Alexander heard this,
he was greatly disturbed
and set off in haste to the capital,
to Antioch.

So now there were two kings in Syria,
and they hated each other.

It came as no surprise
to Demetrius's army
that his first order of business
as a new king of Syria
was to go to war.
What surprised them was
that the war he planned
was not against Alexander,
but against the Jews!

Demetrius appointed Apollonius,
the governor of the province of Coele-Syria,
as general of his army.

Apollonius made headquarters
in Jabneh on the plain.
In a message to Jonathan,
who was in Jerusalem,
Apollonius sent these taunting words:

"Jonathan, you want to fight me
from Jerusalem.
Of what value is your boast

that you are more powerful than I
when you say that
from a mountaintop?

"If you truly believe
you are stronger than I,
come down from Jerusalem,
and once we are both
on the same level field,
we can put your power to the test.
For I have great power on the plain.

"Ask around and learn
what a very important person I am—
and what influential friends I have!
People will tell you
that you cannot put your foot in my face
when your foot and my foot
are standing on the same level ground!

"Your ancestors have twice before
been defeated in their own land.
You shall not withstand
my great army down on the plain,
where there is no advantage of height,
no stones or pebbles to throw,
no place to run and hide!"

Jonathan chose ten thousand troops
and went down from Jerusalem
with his brother Simon beside him.

They pitched their tents near Jaffa,
where Apollonius had a garrison.
Jonathan stormed the city,
whereupon the people
opened wide the gates.
And Jonathan easily took the city.

Jonathan's Victory at Ashdod

When Apollonius heard
that Jonathan had come down
to the plain and captured Jaffa,
he took three thousand cavalry,
with a great army of infantry,
and went to the city of Ashdod
on the plain.
Jonathan and Simon followed.

Now Apollonius sent back toward Jaffa
one thousand of his best cavalry
to ambush Jonathan's army.
He ordered them to hide and wait
in a ravine along the winding road
between Jaffa and Ashdod.

But Jonathan had been forewarned.
So he was able to get his men
to the ravine first.
He ordered them to hide
high in the hills encircling the ravine,

and to stockpile split logs—
firewood—
which they would use as missiles
against the enemy cavalry.

The cavalry trotted into the ravine,
planning to hide and wait
to ambush Jonathan.
Instead, Jonathan's men
already hiding in the hills
began shouting—
announcing their positions.

First, the men on the south hill
began to shout.
The cavalry charged up that hill,
but the horsemen were driven back
by the barrage of firewood
hurled from the hilltop.

Then the men on the north hill
began shouting.
The cavalry turned
and went charging up that hill,
only to face
another barrage of flying firewood
that drove them and their horses
back down into the ravine.

Jonathan's men on the east hill
did the same,
and so did the men on the west.
All the while,

the men not hurling missiles
ran to gather hurled ones,
wherever the wood lay,
to rearm themselves.

And so it went all through the day.
Sticks of firewood
went flying at horses and riders
from morning till evening,
as Jonathan had ordered.
And as Jonathan had expected,
the horses grew tired
from charging up the hills
and running down the hills,
dodging missiles all day long.

Then Simon brought forth his men,
who were fresh
because they had not yet engaged in battle.
He set them against the infantry,
but not against the cavalry,
for he knew the horses were spent—
and the riders, too—
from dodging missiles.

With the cavalry too tired to fight,
Simon could devote all his forces
to defeating the infantry.

The infantry was vanquished.
The cavalry scattered
and galloped for safety

to the temple of Dagon in Ashdod.
The riders took refuge there
and prayed to the image:

"O Dagon, save us from the Jews!
All our troubles are because of the Jews!
O Dagon, show your power!
Destroy them!"

Jonathan set fire to the temple
with the men in it.
Then he plundered Ashdod
and set the city on fire.
Eight thousand enemy
died that day by fire and sword.

The battle of Ashdod
was a great victory
for Jonathan
and a great defeat
for the new Syrian king.

When Jonathan reached Ashkelon,
the news of his victories
had preceded him.
The people came pouring out of the city,
greeting him with shouts
and cheers and applause.
When the cheering stopped,
Jonathan greeted every person;
after clasping the last man's arm,
he went home with horses and other spoils
to Jerusalem.

BALLAD 17
PTOLEMY PHILOMETOR

Ptolemy's Plot

At this time,
Ptolemy Philometor, king of Egypt,
hatched a most deceitful plot
against Alexander, his son-in-law.
Ptolemy knew
Syria now had two kings.
He wished to take advantage
of this situation
to capture Syria
and join it to Egypt.

So Ptolemy assembled a great army
and gathered a great fleet
and marched and sailed
from Egypt to Syria.
He spoke of peace
all along the way.
The people of the cities
opened wide the gates before him
and greeted him
with joy.

As soon as Ptolemy entered a city,
he set up a garrison
and stationed troops there.
No one was suspicious,
because Alexander had told the people
to welcome his father-in-law
as a great king and friend.

As Ptolemy approached Ashdod,
the gentiles and converts,
hoping to make him hate Jonathan,
ran forth to meet him.
They showed him the temple of Dagon,
which Jonathan had burned,
the city of Ashdod
and its neighboring towns,
which Jonathan had destroyed,
the corpses of people
that had been cast forth
from the city and towns,
and the remains of the soldiers,
gathered in heaps
along the king's way.

They fully expected the king
to condemn Jonathan.
But Ptolemy said nothing.

Later that day
Jonathan met Ptolemy at Jaffa
with great ceremony.
Knowing nothing of Ptolemy's intentions,
Jonathan welcomed him

because he was the father-in-law
of Jonathan's dear friend, Alexander.
They embraced
and praised each other.

That evening
Jonathan hosted
a banquet in the king's honor,
and that night he provided him
with luxurious lodging.
The next day,
Jonathan escorted Ptolemy
as far as the Eleutherus River.
And then Jonathan,
thoroughly deceived by the king,
returned home to Jerusalem.

Ptolemy, on arriving by ship
at Seleucia-by-the-Sea,
sent emissaries
to Demetrius saying,

"Let us make an alliance,
and I will give you
my daughter in marriage,
the one who is now married
to Alexander,
and you shall reign unopposed
in your father's kingdom.

"It was a mistake for me
to have given my daughter

313

to Alexander,
for he is plotting to kill me."

Thus did Ptolemy slander Alexander
because he wanted his kingdom.
And Alexander
knew nothing of the slander
because he was away in Cilicia
quashing a rebellion.

Ptolemy's daughter loved Alexander
and adored their little boy,
young Antiochus,
who looked just like his father
and had the same mannerisms.

When Ptolemy told his daughter
that Alexander was trying to kill him,
she looked at him quizzically
and said,
"Dearest Father, you are mistaken.
Alexander loves you
as much as I love you,
and if it were possible, even more."

Ptolemy replied,
"You shall marry the man I choose.
There need be no divorce,
for you've never been married.
And you have no children,
for we will send your son into exile.
So let us prepare at once
for a new wedding.

The surgeons will even
make you a virgin again."

The woman wailed.
Just then young Antiochus
came running into the room.
He embraced his grandfather
with hugs and kisses,
and climbed into his lap—
he was so happy to see him.

Ptolemy called for his men,
who dragged the boy away,
struggling and screaming.
He sent his grandson
to his friend Emalqu, the Arabian,
to raise as his own son
in Emalqu's home.

Then Ptolemy arranged a wedding
for his daughter and Demetrius II.
Thus did Ptolemy
abandon his son-in-law Alexander
and embrace Demetrius
as his new son-in-law.

Now the Syrians hated Demetrius II,
not only because he was
the son of a hated father, Demetrius I,
but especially because
the very first thing he had done as king
was to wage an unnecessary war

against the Jews
and suffer a humiliating defeat
by them at Ashdod.

Ptolemy entered Antioch in triumph.
Alexander was away,
and his throne was empty.

So Ptolemy took a seat
on Alexander's throne,
and set Alexander's crown upon his head.
Ptolemy was now king of Syria
as well as Egypt,
and his new son-in-law, King Demetrius,
was under him.

Things had turned out
just as Ptolemy wished.

The Deaths of Alexander and Ptolemy

When Alexander
learned these things in Cilicia,
he became enraged
at Ptolemy, his father-in-law.
Their mutual enmity
became known to all.

Alexander left Cilicia
and marched against Ptolemy.
But Ptolemy's army was too strong.

316

So Alexander fled into Arabia,
where some Arabs gave him refuge
and defended him.

But Ptolemy of Egypt
was greatly admired in Arabia.
Zabdiel, an Arabian,
on learning of the conflict and enmity
between Alexander and Ptolemy,
cut off Alexander's head
and sent it to Ptolemy
in a silver box.
The gift pleased the king greatly.

Three days later
Ptolemy himself was murdered
by men loyal to Demetrius,
for Demetrius all along
had wished to rule his own country.

And so, in the 167th year
of the Kingdom of the Greeks,   [145 B.C.E.]
Demetrius II
was the one and only king of Syria.

BALLAD 18
TRYPHO

Demetrius II Discharges His Army

When Demetrius II saw   [145 B.C.E.]
that he was the sole ruler of Syria,
and Syria was at peace,
and there was no opposition to him,
and all his enemies were dead,
he discharged his armed forces,
every man to his hometown.
He had no intention
of paying salaries
to soldiers he no longer needed.

He kept a small army of mercenaries
whom he had recruited
at minimal wages
from the Islands of the Sea.

The troops in the Citadel
in Jerusalem
and in the fortresses
throughout Judea
he kept at their posts,
for the Jews in Judea,

318

more and more,
were speaking of independence.

He was unaware
or didn't care
that he had incurred
the hatred of the Syrian soldiers
by discharging them
with no further income
from the government.

A Man Named Trypho

There was a man named Trypho,
a Syrian lord,
born into the religion
of Zeus, the Father,
and devoted to the mystery
of Dionysus, the son.
Trypho was a man
of secret and great ambition,
who claimed to have been
a dear friend of Alexander's.

On learning that Demetrius's former soldiers
were speaking badly of their king,
Trypho saw this
as the opportune moment
to set into motion his scheme
to make himself king of Syria.

So he went to Emalqu the Arabian,
who was raising Antiochus,
Alexander's little boy.
Trypho told the Arab
that he was Alexander's dearest friend,
and he beseeched him
to place the boy in his care,
for he said that Alexander,
just before he died,
had appointed Trypho regent.

He also told Emalqu
of the animosity
the Syrian army bore
toward Demetrius.
The army, he said,
and the Syrian people, too,
wanted young Antiochus—
not Demetrius—
to be their king.
That much of his story was true.

Emalqu listened attentively,
but not without suspicion.
So he extended to Trypho
hospitality over several days
to determine whether Trypho
was a man of good character,
for Emalqu was fond of Antiochus,
was protective of him,
and had no intention
of turning him over to anyone.

Young Antiochus, for his part,
loved the Arab,
who had been kind to him,
treating him like a loving father
treats a beloved son,
and had taught him many things,
including how to ride horses
in the desert sands.
Antiochus did not want to leave Emalqu.

During Trypho's visit,
in addition to giving gifts
of gold and silver to Emalqu,
Trypho made a show
of playing with the boy
and giving him gifts of sweets and toys—
miniature soldiers, forts,
and even engines of war—
and was highly attentive to him.

At the end of the visit,
Emalqu was satisfied.
Trypho had passed the test.
The Arab was deceived.

Emalqu told Antiochus
that going with Trypho was best,
for that was what his father had wanted.
So Emalqu bid Antiochus farewell,
and with tears in their eyes
let Antiochus go.

Jonathan Saves Demetrius

In the meantime,
Jonathan
sent a letter to Demetrius,
saying,

"If you are truly my friend,
as you claim to be,
then discharge the troops
in the Citadel
and those in the fortresses
throughout Judea
and recall them to Syria."

Demetrius responded,
"Yes, of course,
I will do whatever you ask,
and I will honor you
in every way—
whenever the occasion arises.
For now, however, I need your help:
Send fighting men at once.
My whole army has turned against me
and is fomenting revolution."

On hearing this,
Jonathan sent to Antioch
three thousand able-bodied
young Jews to help Demetrius.

When Jonathan's men
were announced,

the king was very happy,
for the Jews hadn't arrived
a moment too soon.

In the center of the city,
one hundred twenty thousand Antiochians
had gathered to kill the king.
They barricaded the streets
and began to riot.

A platoon of Jews
guarded the palace
to protect the king,
while companies of Jewish men
spread throughout the city.
That day in the city of Antioch
Jonathan's men killed
one hundred thousand Antiochians
and regained control
of the town
for Demetrius.

When the Antiochians
saw Jews occupying their city
and looting and burning buildings,
they became disheartened
and went to the king
in humility,
contrite and in tears.
They cast down their arms
and pleaded,

"Great King,
be merciful and do not punish us,
and we will never do this again,
but will serve you faithfully
even without pay.
Only make the Jews stop attacking us!"

The king was merciful,
but at the same time,
addressing the crowd,
he praised the Jews
for coming to his rescue.

Then the Jews returned to Jerusalem,
laden with spoils,
gifts from the king.

So Demetrius continued to sit
on the throne of his kingdom,
and there was peace in his land.

No longer having need of the Jews,
his feelings toward them changed.
He forgot all the things
they had done—
including saving his life.
He forgot his promise
to discharge the men in the Citadel
and from the forts throughout Judea.

Instead,
Demetrius began to slander Jonathan,
saying,

"The Jew cannot be trusted.
He sent his men for the reward,
for the silver and gold,
and not to help me.
And I could have won
easily
without him!"

As the prophet said,
"The heart is deceitful above all things,
and desperately corrupt.
Who can know it?"

Trypho Deposes Demetrius

By this time
Trypho had returned from Arabia
with Alexander's young son Antiochus,
who was wearing the crown.

Demetrius's army
now gathered round Trypho
and Antiochus, the young king,
and pledged allegiance to them.

Antiochus's first order as king
was to capture Demetrius.
So the army went to the palace in Antioch.
There they routed the mercenaries,
and Demetrius fled.

The Friendship of Antiochus and Jonathan

Antiochus wrote a letter
to Jonathan saying,

"As my father, Alexander,
did before me,
I confirm you
as high priest of your people,
appoint you ruler of Judea,
and want you to be
one of the king's friends."

Along with his letter,
the king sent many gifts,
including beautiful gold goblets.
And he requested
that Jonathan
drink from them
in the manner of kings,
and that he clothe himself
in purple, the color of kings,
and wear a gold buckle
as kings do.

Antiochus appointed
Jonathan's brother Simon
governor of the land of Judea
from the outskirts of Tyre
all the way
to the Egyptian border.

The Routing of Demetrius's Army

Jonathan heard that officers loyal to Demetrius
had come with an army of mercenaries
to the city of Kadesh in Galilee
with the intent of killing Jonathan.
So Jonathan marched into Galilee
and pitched camp
on the shores of Lake Kinneret,
whose waters were fresh and sweet,
but which the gentiles called
the Sea of Galilee.

Early in the morning
Jonathan and his men
went out on the plain of Hazor.
The mercenary army,
hiding in the mountains,
came charging onto the plain,
ambushing them.

Terrified, all of Jonathan's men fled
except two—
Judah ben Calphi
and Mattathias ben Absalom,
loyal and brave men,
both of them captains.

Deserted by all but two,
Jonathan felt bereft—
like a man in mourning.
He rent his clothing,

327

cast earth upon his head,
and prayed in words of David,

"O grant us help
against the foe,
for vain is the help of man!
With you at our side
we shall do valiantly!"

Jonathan and his two captains—
three men in all!—
returned to fight
and, hard as it is to believe,
put the enemy to flight!

When the Jewish deserters saw this,
they were ashamed
and rejoined Jonathan,
who welcomed them gladly.
They pursued the enemy
into the city of Kadesh,
into their camp
and into their tents,
where they slew them.

Three thousand mercenaries
died that day.
Then Jonathan returned home
to Jerusalem.

Calling On the Romans

Now Jonathan Apphus
decided the time had come
to call on
his old friends and allies
the Romans.

He sent two emissaries
to confirm and renew
the friendship
between Judea and Rome.

The emissaries entered Rome,
walked into the Senate,
and said:

"Jonathan, high priest of the Jews,
along with the entire nation,
has sent us to Rome
for the purpose
of renewing
our old friendship and alliance."

On hearing this,
the Romans smiled and nodded,
and gave them
letters of safe passage
back to Judea.

Jonathan Prepares for Battle

In the meantime
Demetrius had raised
another army of mercenaries,
greater than the one before,
and had marched toward Judea,
as far as the Galilean border.

When Jonathan heard
that Demetrius was on the march
and intent on invading Judea,
he left Jerusalem
and met the enemy
in the land of Hamath.

Jonathan sent spies
into the enemy camp.
They returned and reported
that the enemy
was planning to attack
during the night.

So as soon as the sun went down,
Jonathan ordered his men
to keep watch, to be alert,
to have their arms ready
all through the night.
And he stationed sentries round about.

When the enemy heard
that Jonathan had been forewarned,
they became alarmed.

They lighted campfires
to pretend they were still in camp,
and then they slipped away.

Jonathan did not learn this
until morning,
when he saw the campfires burning
but the camp deserted.

He set off in pursuit
but could not catch them,
for they had already crossed
the river Eleutherus.
Moreover, at the river,
Jonathan encountered
a tribe of Zabadeans,
Arabs hostile to Jews.
He attacked, defeated,
and plundered them.
Then Jonathan returned to Jerusalem.

Isolating the Citadel

As soon as Jonathan
entered the City of David,
he called an assembly
of the elders of the people.

They decided to encircle the Citadel
with a wall,

a great ring of high-mounded earth,
to isolate it,
so that those inside the Citadel,
having no access to the city,
would eventually starve.

Trypho Sets a Trap

Trypho was determined
to conquer all the kingdoms
and provinces of the East,
then to kill Antiochus
and place the crown
on his own head.
But Trypho feared
that Jonathan would thwart his plans,
for Jonathan had supported Alexander
and would surely support his son.
So Trypho was determined
to capture and kill Jonathan first.

Jonathan was at home in Jerusalem.
He had spent the morning
planting and watering crops
with Jesus and Jonas, his sons.
Part of the afternoon
he played with his baby daughter;
part he spent reading
his treasured copy of the *Iliad*;
and part he spent with Rachel, his wife,
the bride of his youth, his best friend.

Rachel and Jonathan loved each other
even more than on that first day in the cave.
One soul, one heart, one mind
between two!
Nothing is better or more precious,
particularly when two as one
run a household together
as husband and wife.
And so it was with Jonathan and Rachel.

This day
Jonathan was particularly overcome
with desire.
He said in words of Torah,
"Rachel was beautiful and lovely,"
and in words from the Song of Songs,
"Behold, you are beautiful, my love,
behold, you are beautiful."

Then he said,
"You are, without any doubt,
the most beautiful woman
in the world."

Rachel laughed and said,
"Surpassing Aphrodite?"

"Surpassing Helen of Troy!
And I've never wanted you more!"
Jonathan drew her to him
and kissed her hard upon the lips.

No sooner had they slipped
into their bed of joy,
than there came
a loud knocking at the door.

Jonathan put on his robe
and opened the door.
Aeneas, one of his captains,
was standing there and said,
"Abba, I am sorry to interrupt you,
but I have bad news.
Trypho is on the march."

Jonathan said,
"Trypho is the guardian of the king,
the son of Alexander,
our greatest friend
among the gentiles.
The young king is our friend, too,
just as his father was.
Trypho comes in peace."

Rachel said,
"The day Trypho comes
with an army in peace
is the day we will surely
be destroyed.
What is peace to Trypho,
but to acquiesce to him,
to die willingly before him,
or to go eagerly into slavery?"

334

Aeneas resumed,
"Trypho has marched
to Beth-Shean."

Jonathan,
on the advice of Aeneas
and Rachel,
took a great army
and marched to meet Trypho.
When Trypho saw Jonathan
with forty thousand
of the finest Jewish warriors,
he didn't lift a finger against him.

Instead,
Trypho received Jonathan
warmly and respectfully,
praised him endlessly,
introduced him shamelessly
as one of his dearest friends,
and lavished gifts upon him
abundantly.
He ordered his soldiers
to obey Jonathan
as they would obey himself.

Trypho said,
"Jonathan Apphus,
why have you gone to the trouble
of raising such a great army for war
when there is nothing

for us to fight about?
Abba, my dearest friend,
send your troops home,
except for a few attendants,
and join me in Acre
that I may turn it over to you,
along with its fortress
and the soldiers in charge.

"I myself shall go to Acre at once
to make preparations
to receive you properly.
It was to tell you these things
that I came here."

Jonathan set aside all wariness,
but his captain
took him aside
and said,
"Abba, this man is a liar.
How can you trust him?"

Jonathan placed an arm
around Aeneas's shoulder,
smiled, and said,
"Aeneas, not only
are you a good soldier
and a good officer,
but you are a dear and loyal friend.
You always give me good advice.
But on this matter,
let me tell you something.
Unless people begin

to trust one another,
how can there ever be peace?
Besides,
Trypho is the servant
of my old friend Alexander
and the regent and guardian
of Alexander's son.
So Trypho is surely a friend."

Long wars, despair,
and repeated frustration
fill the most intelligent of men
with blind hope for peace.
Such hope only grows stronger
as the enemy tells the same lies
over and over again.

And so Jonathan did
exactly as Trypho had requested.
He sent most of his army home,
but kept a company of three thousand.
Of these, he sent two thousand
into Galilee,
to the great plain just beyond Acre,
and one thousand he kept at his side.

Then Jonathan went to Acre.
On nearing the gates of the city,
he was amazed to see
a royal reception awaiting him.
A red carpet had been spread
all the way to the city gates,

and trumpeters were stationed
along the way
sounding fanfares.
Jonathan was overcome.

So he sent away
most of the one thousand men
and gave them orders to join those
who had assembled
on the great plain of Galilee.
He kept but a few of his soldiers
at his side.

The gates of Acre opened,
and Jonathan entered the city
accompanied by his small retinue.
Fanfares sounded within the city,
followed by great cheering of crowds,
and the whole town
was decked in splendor.
Jonathan was astonished
and exceedingly moved.
He was being treated like a gentile king
returning home from war in triumph!

Then
Trypho's troops locked the gates.
They surrounded Jonathan,
arrested him,
and slew his men
by the sword.

Then Trypho sent a great army
of infantry and cavalry
to the plain of Galilee
to massacre Jonathan's company,
which was taken by surprise.

They slew them all and rejoiced.
Then they prepared for more conflict.

Simon Becomes Leader of the Jews

When the Jews were told
that Jonathan had been captured
and murdered with all his men—
that was the earliest report—
they wept and wailed
and were very much afraid.
And all Israel mourned
in bitter lamentation.

Then all the gentiles
living round about
sought to destroy Israel completely,
saying,

"They have no leader.
The time is ripe
to annihilate them
and to wipe out
all memory of the Jews

from the minds of men
forever."

When Simon heard
that Trypho had raised a mighty army
to invade the land of Judea
and destroy it completely,
and when he saw the Jews
so distressed and trembling with fear,
he went up to Jerusalem,
where he called the people together
and spoke encouraging words:

"Countrymen, fellow Jews,
you all know the things
my brothers and I
and all my father's house
have done to win religious liberty,
so that we may study Torah,
keep the Covenant
and the commandments,
preserve the Temple,
and worship freely and untroubled.

"You know the campaigns we fought,
the hardships we endured,
and how all my brothers died
for Israel's sake.
I am the only one left,
the last of the sons of Mattathias,
and it is not my intention
to spare my own life
at this time of great trouble and danger.

For I am no more worthy of life
than my brave brothers.

"The nations of the gentiles
have gathered together
to rise up against us,
to make war upon us
and destroy us
out of malice.
They hate us
simply because we are Jews—
a people whose only wish
is to live in peace.

"My father and my brothers
have not died in vain.
The righteous shall prevail,
and the wicked shall disappear.
And there shall be peace everlasting
upon the earth
and goodwill among all the peoples.
In the words of Micah,
'And none shall make them afraid.'

"Children of Israel,
I pledge to you
that I shall work toward these goals
all the days of my life."

As soon as the people
heard these words,
their spirit revived.

And they responded
in a loud voice, saying,

"Simon, son of Mattathias,
you are our leader now,
to take the place of your brothers
Jonathan Abba
and Judah Maccabee.

"Carry on!
Fight the good fight!
Fight for liberty and fight for us!
Whatever you command,
we will do."

So Simon assembled
the finest warriors
and placed Jonathan ben Absalom
in charge of an army,
which he sent to Jaffa
to cast out the enemy there.
And Simon took command
of the remaining warriors
to defend and protect Jerusalem.

More of Trypho's Treachery

Meanwhile,
Trypho marched from Acre
with his great army
to invade Judea.

Jonathan was with him,
imprisoned in a cage
and under guard.

When Trypho learned
that Simon was the new leader
and had taken Jonathan's place,
Trypho sent messengers to Simon,
saying,

"Jonathan is not dead.
We have imprisoned him
because he owes money
to the king's treasury—
payment due for the offices he held.

"We will release him
if you send
one hundred talents of silver
and his two sons as hostages,
to ensure that when he is released
he does not incite Judea
to make war upon me and my king."

Even though Simon knew
that Trypho's messengers
were speaking treachery,
he decided to send the money
and Jonathan's sons,
lest he win the enmity of those
who would surely say,

"Because Simon did not send
the money and the children,
Jonathan has been killed!"

Simon went to Jonathan's home
and spoke to Rachel,
Jonathan's wife and the mother of his children.
They were in mourning for Jonathan.
Simon explained
the unexpected change of circumstances.
"Jonathan is still alive,
a prisoner held by Trypho.
Papa is alive!
Do you understand?"

Rachel replied,
"It cannot be true!
Papa is dead!"

"No! Jonathan is alive,
and Trypho demands
that we send the boys,
Jesus and Jonas,
or Trypho will kill him."

The distraught woman replied,
"Trypho is setting another trap!
If Jonathan were truly dead,
it would not hurt so much
as the news you now bring.
I am already in mourning for Jonathan.
Must I mourn for him
a second time?

And must I go into mourning
for his sons?
No! No! No!"

"We must send the boys,
or Trypho will kill Jonathan!"

"Then, Simon, you go—
or send John or Judah
or Mattathias or Jason,
your sons—
but not my sons!"

"Rachel, you don't understand!
Trypho will accept
only Papa's sons."

Jesus said, "Mama,
we cannot let Papa die!
What are you thinking?"

"What am I *thinking*?
This is what I am thinking!
It is more important
for my sons to live—
for Jonathan's sons to live!—
than to ransom their father,
whom I love more than life.
You boys must live
so that you
can carry on
your father's work—

and your grandfather's
and your uncle's—
your uncle Judah Maccabee!

"If your father is really alive,
you know he would agree with me.

"Simon, you know
Jonathan would agree with me!

"A father may be a ransom for a son,
but no son may be a ransom for a father!
And that monster demands two sons!
No! No! No!
Papa would never want that!
Judah Maccabee
would never permit that!
Never! Never! Never!"

And Rachel began to weep and sob,
because she knew
her speech was in vain.

Simon said to her, "Not a ransom!
Hostages!
The boys will only be hostages,
to guarantee that Jonathan,
on his release,
does not attack Trypho."

Jesus placed an arm
around his mother
and kissed her on the brow and cheeks.

"Mama, you said it was important
for Jonas and me
to carry on Papa's work.
If we go now,
we will enable Papa
to carry on Papa's work!"

Simon said, "Rachel,
your sons' childhood days are over.
They are already big and strong.
They don't need you
to make decisions for them
anymore."

Jonas said, "Well, it's decided then!"

Jesus said, "Uncle Simon, will Trypho
make us eat pork?"

Simon responded,
"I don't know what he will make you do.
But whatever it is, do it.
Otherwise, he will surely kill you.

"When we are attacked
on the Sabbath,
we fight on the Sabbath;
and God forgives us for doing so.
The Creator does not want us to die
for the sake of our religion.
The Creator wants us to live
so we can celebrate our religion

and enjoy the meaningful life it gives us.
God will forgive you,
whatever Trypho makes you do,
for anything done under force
is not evil.
It is force itself that is evil."

The Death of Jonathan

Then Simon sent Jonathan's sons
along with the money
to Trypho.

When they arrived,
Trypho sent this message back to Simon:
"Even though you have sent
the hostages and the money,
I have decided not to let Jonathan go."

Trypho kept the money,
violated Jonathan's sons,
and slew them.
Then he tossed the corpses
into a ravine
to be eaten by wild animals
and carrion birds.

Then he visited Jonathan in his cage.
He beat him,
and then he told him
everything he'd done.

348

After Trypho did
these abominable things,
he invaded Judea,
intent on destroying it.
He went a roundabout way,
by the road that leads to Adora,
for it was his plan
to lay siege to Jerusalem.

Simon and his army tracked him.
They were determined
to destroy Trypho
no matter where he went.

Meanwhile,
the enemy in the Citadel
had run out of food
and sent this message to Trypho:
"Come as quickly as you can
by the desert route,
and bring us food,
for we are starving to death."

Trypho prepared cavalry and provisions
to leave that very night.
But there was a snowstorm,
making travel to Jerusalem
impossible.

Trypho had no more time
to worry about the men

in the Citadel.
Now his thoughts turned entirely
toward advancing his plan
of becoming king.
So he went toward Gilead
where, according to the report,
the air was cold
but the sun was shining.
When he drew near
the city of Bascama,
he made camp.

Then he visited Jonathan in his cage.

Jonathan,
his eyes red, his cheeks moist,
his voice hoarse to a soft whisper,
said, "Why have you come?"

"To judge you,
Jonathan Apphus."

"To judge me?"

"To judge you
for your crime."

"My crime?
What is my crime?"

"You are a Jew."

"Yes, that is true.
If that is a crime,
I am guilty."

"That makes things easier—
to hear your confession."

"What is the punishment
for my crime?"

"Only one punishment
fits that crime—death."

Thereupon
Trypho drew his sword
and stabbed Jonathan
through the lower belly.
He moved the sword
steadily upward,
passing the navel,
and when the sword
struck the breastbone,
it came to a halt.
Then Trypho slowly
withdrew the sword.

All the while
Trypho was cutting Jonathan,
Abba did not utter a sound.
Trypho was amazed
by the silence.
He had never seen anything like it.

It surpassed the sacrifice
of an ox or a pig
at the altar of the gods.

One of Trypho's officers,
a converted Jew,
was so moved that he said aloud
the words of the prophet,

"He was wounded
for our transgressions. . . .
And YHV has laid on him
the iniquity of us all.
He was oppressed and afflicted,
yet he opened not his mouth,
like a lamb
that is led to the slaughter."

The officer continued,
"Behold my servant,
whom I uphold, my chosen,
in whom my soul delights!
I have breathed my spirit into him.
He will bring forth justice
to the gentiles.
He shall not cry,
nor lift up his voice."

The red blood spurted
as Jonathan's life poured out of him.
Trypho shouted for a goblet.
An officer brought him one,
and Trypho caught the blood

in the goblet and drank it,
for he was certain
there was something more sacred here
than the mystery of Dionysus.

Then Trypho did something strange.
He took a shovel,
broke ground,
and dug a grave.
And he buried Jonathan respectfully,
as if he were a member
of his own family
or his best friend.
After he buried him,
Trypho did the strangest thing of all.
He began to mourn Jonathan,
weeping, calling his name
over and over again,
"Apphus! Apphus! Apphus!"

Trypho's officers and soldiers
were embarrassed.
His adjutant said,
"General, why are you
behaving like this over a Jew?"

Trypho responded,
"Jonathan Apphus
was more than a Jew.
Jonathan Apphus was a god."

"But General, you despise the Jews.
Besides, how can a Jew be a god?"

"I despise the gods!
Only a Jew is worthy to be a god.
They call themselves
the sons of God."

His adjutant said,
"And you believe it?"

Trypho fell to his knees,
threw dirt upon his head
and upon his body,
and began to sob and shake,
to wail and quake.

Suddenly
he ran to his tent.
There, composed,
he sat down at his table
and wrote a message to Simon,
telling him where in Bascama
he had buried Jonathan.

Then Trypho
returned to Antioch,
for he had one more job to do
before his plan
was accomplished.

Jonathan's Funeral

Simon went to Bascama
and found the place
where Jonathan was buried.
It was just where Trypho had said.
He gathered the remains
and took them to Modin
and buried them there,
in Modin,
the town of his ancestors.   [143 B.C.E.]

Simon prayed,
"Almighty God,
grant your peace
and your everlasting love
to my brother,
to the soul of Jonathan Abba,
who has entered into eternity.
May he share
in the glory of the righteous
that shines
like the stars in heaven."

The trumpet sounded,
"Ta RA, ta RA, ta RAA."
And all Israel
made great lamentation
over Jonathan
for many days.

355

Simon built a great monument
by the graves of his parents
and his brothers.
It was so high
it could be seen
at a great distance,
and it was made of quarried stone
polished on all sides.

The monument had seven pyramids
all in a row:
one for his father,
one for his mother,
and one for each of his four brothers,
all dead.
The seventh pyramid was for himself,
when the time came.

And the monument had a porch
with columns round about,
and over the columns was a frieze
showing in high relief
the engines of war used by his brothers
and also the suits of armor worn by them.
Their names were inscribed there, too.

Also on the frieze were ships,
a delight to men who sail the sea,
and a reminder of the harbor at Jaffa,
so dear to Simon's heart.

This was the monument
that Simon built at Modin

in honor and memory
of his family.

Simon was the last
of the sons of Mattathias.

Trypho, King of the East

Now Trypho
dealt treacherously and abominably
with the young king, Antiochus,
Alexander's son,
and slew him.

He announced to the world
that Antiochus had fallen ill,
and that the surgeon who cared for him
had bled him to death.

Then Trypho,
with great pomp and ceremony,
crowned himself king of the East.
With the gold crown on his head,
Trypho had accomplished
all he had set out to do.
But his reign as king of Syria
brought only disaster
to that country.

BALLAD 19
INDEPENDENCE

Judea's Declaration of Independence

And so it was
that in the 170th year
of the Kingdom of the Greeks,   [142 B.C.E.]
with the departure of Trypho,
the yoke of the Greeks
was lifted from Israel,
and Simon declared Judea
an independent nation.

Simon wrote to Demetrius II,
telling him that he recognized him,
not Trypho, as king of Syria.
Demetrius was the lesser of two evils.
And Demetrius responded,
recognizing Simon as high priest
and recognizing the nation of the Jews:

> From King Demetrius
> to Simon, the high priest
> and friend of kings,
> and also to the elders
> and to the nation of the Jews:

BALLAD 19: INDEPENDENCE

Greetings!
We have received your gift
of a gold crown . . . ,
and we wish to make
a lasting peace with you,
and to write to our officials
to confirm the privileges
we have granted you.

We guarantee that all the treaties
we have made with you shall stand,
and all the fortresses
you have built are yours.

Any oversights or debts
committed against us—
even up to this very day—
we forgive them all,
even the crown tax that is our due.

Tributes you used to pay
in Jerusalem
shall be collected no more.

Select your worthiest men
to serve in our palace court,
and send them here
that we may enroll them.
And let there be peace between us.

Then Simon built up Judea.

The people of Israel
began to conduct business
as in ancient days
and to make contracts.
They wrote in their documents
that this transaction took place
"in the first year of Simon
the high priest,
commander in chief,
and leader of the Jews."

A new era had begun.
After long centuries of oppression,
the children of Israel
were liberated.
And Judea, the land of the Jews,
was an independent nation
once more.

The Capture of Gaza

In those days,
Simon camped
near the walls of Gaza,
and his troops besieged it on all sides.
They made engines of war
for battering towers.
The soldiers in the engines
leaped over the walls into the city
and opened the city gates.

BALLAD 19: INDEPENDENCE

The men of Gaza
rent their clothing,
climbed to the top of the city walls
with their wives and children,
and begged Simon
to stop the attack
and grant them peace,
shouting,

"Forgive us, and treat us
not in accordance
with the terrible things
we've done to the Jews,
but in accordance
with your mercy!"

Simon was merciful.
He did not kill them,
but he did make them
leave the city.
Then he cleansed their houses,
which held idols,
removed all the pollution,
and entered the city
with happy songs
and thanksgiving.

And Simon
built his home
in Gaza
and dwelled there.

The Fall of the Citadel

Abandoned by Trypho,
the enemy soldiers
in the Citadel
were in dire straits,
for they were starving.
Many had already perished
from famine.
The survivors
called out to Simon
that they wished
to surrender.

Simon carried the soldiers
from the Citadel
and cleansed it of pollution.
He leveled the ring
of high-mounded earth round about it.

He nourished the soldiers
back to health
and let them return
to their own countries.
The converted Jews
chose to go with the gentiles,
for they had done too much harm
to the faithful Jews
to remain.

With the fall of the Citadel,
the last stronghold
of foreign occupation

in all Judea came to an end,
and Jerusalem at last
was completely free.
Her wars on behalf
of religious liberty
and an independent nation
were accomplished.

As the prophet said,
"'Comfort my people,
comfort them,'
says your God.
'Speak tenderly to Jerusalem,
and cry to her
that her warfare is over,
that her iniquity is pardoned.'"

Simon's Triumphal Entry into Jerusalem

Simon entered Jerusalem
on the twenty-third day
of the second month
in the 171st year
of the Kingdom of the Greeks.   [141 B.C.E.]

He entered the City of David
with thanksgiving,
with the waving of palm fronds
and the playing of harps,
cymbals, and lyres,

and the singing of hymns and songs,
and the dancing of the people
in the streets.

And the people sang words of the prophet:
"How beautiful upon the mountains
are the feet of him who brings good news,
who announces peace,
who brings good news of good,
who announces salvation,
who says to Zion,
'Your God reigns.'"

"'The mountains
shall disappear from the earth
and the hills shall vanish, too,
but my never-ending love
and my covenant of peace
shall never go away from you,'
says YHV,
who has mercy on you."

Simon set up headquarters and barracks
on the Temple Mount.

Because he saw that his son John—
named for his brother John Gaddi—
had grown into brave
and competent manhood,
Simon made him general of all the armies.

And John made his home
in Gezer.

Peace in Judea

And there was peace in Judea.
And the land was plowed
all the days of Simon.

Simon sought only
the good of his nation.
So the people honored him,
respected him,
and chose him to be their ruler
all the days of his life.

And the people sang,

"Great is YHV
and greatly to be praised
in the city of our God.
His holy mountain,
beautiful in elevation,
is the joy of all the earth—
Mount Zion. . . ."

"And the glory of YHV
shall be revealed,
and all flesh
shall see it together,
for the mouth of YHV
has spoken."

In Jaffa,
Simon built a magnificent harbor,

one of his greatest accomplishments.
He made Jaffa the gateway
to the Mediterranean
and to the Islands of the Sea.

Simon liked to sit on the shore at Jaffa,
gazing out to sea
or looking at the ships
docked in the harbor.
He liked watching the boats sail in,
seeing the men on the docks
loading and unloading cargo,
and watching the boats sail away.
Ships in full sail
flying over the blue sea
filled his heart with joy.

Simon recovered the lost territories,
and he gathered into the land
prisoners of war,
refugees,
and former slaves.

Old men sat at tables
in the town squares,
drinking wine mixed with water,
peeling and eating fruit,
chatting and discussing
the questions of the day:

"How long do you think
peace will last?"

"Until a gentile king
rises up against us."

"Why do the gentiles
hate us so?"

"Because we worship
an invisible god,
and they believe only in gods
they can see.
So they worship idols,
and they worship men—
lords and kings
whom they idolize and adore
and make into gods."

"They hate us
because we are honest,
outspoken, direct.
We speak our minds,
while they are circumspect, tactful,
and hide their real thoughts
and feelings."

"They hate us
because we call ourselves
the sons of God
and call God *our* Father
instead of *the* Father."

"They accuse us of blasphemy
because to them

only Dionysus
is the son of God."

"They hate us
because we call ourselves
the chosen people."

"But the Torah does say:
'You are the sons of YHV your God . . .
YHV has chosen you
to be a people for his own possession.'"

"But the gentiles don't know
a word of Torah!"

"No words of Torah, it seems, but these."

"But they are figures of speech."

"Some of our people take them literally—
especially the pious."

"And the gentiles do, too."

"They hate us
because they envy and admire us."

"That makes no sense,
for if that is true,
they should love us!"

"Envy and admiration bring hate,
not love."

"Why do the gentiles
lie about us?"

"Because they cannot destroy us
with truth."

"Do you believe
in the coming of a messiah,
a herald who is to announce
the good news
of an end to war,
the beginning of eternal peace
upon the earth,
and goodwill
among all the peoples?"

"No, the people from Gilead
started that rumor.
They said Elijah their kinsman
would descend from heaven
in a whirlwind or in a chariot of fire,
and then
the messiah would come."

"The prophet Malachi said that
before the people of Gilead ever did."

"Peace on earth
and goodwill among men
are beautiful thoughts,
but I don't believe
in the coming of a messiah,

and neither does Simon,
the high priest!"

"Malachi also said
that when Elijah comes
children will stop fighting
with their parents."

"I'll believe in eternal peace
and goodwill among men
when I see it—
and so will everyone else!"

"I'll believe in eternal peace
when my own children
stop fighting with me!"

And all the men laughed.

"The gentiles resent
our not working on the Sabbath."

"They think we are boasting
that we can do as much work
in six days
as they do in seven—
and get a holiday, too!"

"Why can't Jews and gentiles
share a meal of bread and wine,
vegetables and fruits,
milk and honey?"

"We can.
But then they accuse us
of controlling the meal."

"And according to them,
it's only a step
from controlling the meal
to controlling the world!"

"We encourage our people
to read and write,
but the gentile kings
think reading and writing
are dangerous,
so they keep their people
in ignorance."

"Why do the Greeks
insist on forcing their religion
on everyone else?"

"The gentiles want everyone
to believe the same."

"That is why they call their religion
inclusive,
while ours they call
exclusive."

"They believe
that only they
have the truth.

And they believe
that forcing that 'truth' on others
is good for the people."

"Yes, they see themselves
as the benefactors of humanity
no matter how many people
they hurt or kill
while bestowing their gifts."

"They believe
obedience
is the greatest of virtues.
We believe
disobedience to evil
is a great virtue."

"We boast that our religion
is one of love, mercy,
and forgiveness."

"For us to say such things
implies that the gentiles do not
know such human things.
That is to slander them
as they slander us!"

"Does it matter whether
one calls God
Creator or *Zeus*?"

"Yes, it matters!
Zeus is not a creator;

Zeus was begotten,
and Zeus begets—
like a man or a horse
or a dog."

"The Creator was not created.
The Creator is eternal.
And the Creator does not beget."

"Is there a hereafter?"

"No one has ever come back to tell!"

"Dionysus, son of Zeus,
promises his believers
eternal life."

"Yes, but does he
keep his promise?"

"His believers are so afraid of death,
they fear to doubt him."

"But anyone can promise
eternal life.
Even I can!"

"Will you keep your promise?"

"Of course!"

And all the men laughed.

"Is it good for our government
to be run by the high priest?"

"It's no good at all.
The priests should run religion,
and the governors
should run the government!"

"Tell that to the priests!"

"All our ideas about liberty, tolerance,
and respect for differences
are alien to the gentiles."

"They ridicule them
and call them *Jewish!*"

"How long do you think the Greeks
will remain in power?"

"Until the Romans come
and conquer the Greeks!"

"Last night I dreamed about the Romans.
I awoke with terrifying fear,
drenched in sweat,
my heart wildly beating.
Roman legions were marching,
tramping, invading Judea—
wave upon wave of Romans
coming endlessly.
Young Jewish men

ran out of their homes
to meet each wave of Romans,
but the waves kept coming.
And with each new wave,
there were fewer Jews—
until, when the last wave
rolled upon the shore,
there was not a single Jew to be seen.
Then, in the distance,
I saw a man walking toward me,
shouting words of liberty."

"Ah! So you see!
A Jew did survive!"

Thus did old Jewish men
while away the afternoons—
chatting at tables.

The women remained at home
running the households—
milking goats, growing vegetables,
cooking meals, raising children.

Young men in their leisure
walked around the city squares,
sometimes dressed like warriors,
flirting and chatting
with young and pretty girls,
who smiled and laughed
at anything they said
and tossed their heads.

Simon's Deeds

Simon upheld justice,
and the earth yielded
in abundance.
The fields were filled
with corn and wheat and barley,
and the pastures and meadows
with sheep and goats and cattle.

The trees in the orchards
were so heavy with fruit
their branches broke,
and the sea yielded fish
in abundance.
There was no starvation,
and the people prospered.

Simon encouraged
development of natural resources
and trade with other nations.

The enemy kings
had all been overthrown.
Even so,
Simon armed the towns
so they could defend themselves
if the need arose.

Simon built
beautiful buildings and parks
in Jerusalem.

He planted trees
along all the streets and thoroughfares.
And the Temple shone like a jewel.
Simon's deeds were proclaimed
to the ends of the earth.
And Israel rejoiced greatly,
singing words of Torah:

"And God brought us into this place
and gave us this land,
a land flowing with milk and honey."

"And I will establish my covenant
between me and you
and your descendants after you
throughout their generations,
for an everlasting covenant,
to be God to you
and to your descendants after you.
And I will give to you
and to your descendants after you
the land of your sojournings,
all the land of Canaan,
for an everlasting possession."

Letters from Rome

Simon sent Numenius to Rome
with a gift of a great shield of gold
weighing one thousand pounds

to confirm the Jewish alliance
with Rome.

On learning that Jonathan had died,
the Romans expressed sorrow,
but on hearing that Simon
had taken Jonathan's place,
they expressed delight.

The Romans wrote letters
to the king of Egypt
and to the kings of all the countries
surrounding the land of the Jews
and as far away as
Halicarnassus, Delos, Cos,
Side, and Sparta.

Here is the letter from Lucius,
the Roman consul,
to Ptolemy, king of Egypt—
a letter similar to the ones
he sent to the other kings:

> From Lucius,
> consul of the people of Rome,
> to King Ptolemy:
> Greetings!

> Ambassadors from the Jews,
> our friends and allies,
> came to us
> to renew their old friendship
> and alliance.

They were sent by Simon,
the high priest,
and by the Jewish people,
and they brought with them
a shield of gold
weighing one thousand pounds.

We thought it sensible, therefore,
to write to kings and countries
to do the Jews no harm
and not to fight them,
neither their cities
nor their country,
nor give aid to their enemies.
We thought it sensible, too,
to accept their gift
of the shield of gold. . . .

And Lucius wrote a special letter
to Simon on tablets of brass,
renewing the friendship
between the Romans and the Jews—
an alliance forged by Simon's brothers
Judah Maccabee and Jonathan Apphus.

These writings were read
in Jerusalem
before a great assembly
of priests, leaders, elders,
and the Jewish people
who had come together

for the purpose of honoring Simon
and memorializing
his father and brothers.

When the people
heard the letters, they said,
"How can we sufficiently thank Simon?
He and his brothers—
the whole house of Mattathias—
have established Israel
and secured her liberty.
They have put our enemies to flight
and have confirmed
the independence
of the Jewish nation."

The first year of Simon's reign
was in the 170th year
of the Kingdom of the Greeks.   [142 B.C.E.]
It was the beginning of a new era.
Judea was an independent nation,
and the coinage minted that year
proclaimed that independence.

Never in all her history
had Israel enjoyed
such an extraordinary measure
of happiness.

"Proclaim liberty
throughout the land
to all its inhabitants."

Simon, High Priest Forever

Then the Jews honored Simon
even more.
In the 172nd year
of the Kingdom of the Greeks,   [140 B.C.E.]
on the eighteenth day of the month of Elul,
in the third year of Simon,
the high priest and prince of Israel,
amidst a great assembly
of the priests and the people
and the elders and the rulers of the nation
the following proclamation was read:

> Insofar as there have been
> so many wars in our country,
> during which, for the protection
> of the Temple and the Torah,
> Simon, the son of Mattathias,
> along with his brothers,
> of the lineage of Joarib,
> by placing themselves in harm's way
> and resisting the enemies of our nation,
> have done the Jewish nation
> a great service
> and brought it glory;
>
> insofar as, even after Jonathan
> united the nation
> and became its high priest,
> when our enemies still prepared
> to invade the nation, to destroy it,

and to lay hands upon the Temple,
Simon rose up
and fought for our nation,
spending much of his own fortune
to arm the brave men of his people,
to pay them wages,
to fortify Beth-Zur
and all the cities that border Judea,
places where enemy armies once stood,
to set up garrisons of Jews
to fortify Jaffa, which lies upon the sea,
and Gezer, which borders on Ashdod—
cities where our enemies used to dwell—
and to settle Jews there
and provide them with everything necessary
to maintain these cities;

therefore the Jewish people,
seeing the worthy deeds of Simon
and the glory he has brought to our nation,
have made him their leader and high priest.

Simon did all these things,
all the while preserving justice,
never losing faith in his nation,
and keeping ever foremost in his mind
the exaltation of his people.

During his rule
our nation has prospered,
and those who would destroy us
have been cast away,
including those who were

in the ancient City of David
in Jerusalem,
where they had made themselves
a Citadel,
from which they came forth
to pollute the Temple
and defile everything
round about that holy place.

It was Simon who settled Jews
once more in Jerusalem
and in the ancient City of David,
who built up the walls,
who fortified the city,
and who made it and the nation safe.

The Jewish people appointed Simon
high priest for life
and his sons after him,
until such time
as there should arise once more
an unmistakable prophet in Israel.

King Demetrius heard these things.
He also heard that
the Romans had called the Jews
their friends, allies, and brothers.
So Demetrius also honored Simon.
He reaffirmed Simon as high priest
and made him one of his friends.

Simon accepted the appointments
as high priest,
commander in chief,
leader of the Jews,
and defender of all.

And it was decreed
that his titles should be written
on tablets of brass
and set up in a conspicuous place
within the Temple precincts.

Thus was Simon by popular decree
invested with absolute power,
like a king of the gentile nations.
And thus did Simon become
a hereditary ruler
and the first in a dynasty of high priests.

Simon could not help remembering
the surname his father, Mattathias,
had given him,
Pele yo-etz el gibbor avi-ad sar-shalom,
which means
"A wonderful Counselor is Almighty God,
everlasting Father, Prince of peace."

Simon thought,
"How strange of my father
to bestow upon me
such a name!
What did he have in mind?

"Mattathias believed
in Isaiah and Micah's vision
of everlasting peace
and goodwill among men:

'They shall beat their swords
into plowshares,
and their spears
into pruning hooks.
Nation shall not lift up sword
against nation;
neither shall they learn war
anymore.'

"But Mattathias did not believe
in the coming of the messiah—
no one in my family believed that—
or that God alone
would make the prophets' vision
a reality.

"My father and all my brothers believed,
as I do,
that it is up to mankind,
inspired and guided by God,
to realize the prophets' vision."

Simon prayed,
"Wonderful Counselor,
may you counsel
the leaders of the world
to establish everlasting peace."

BALLAD 20
ANTIOCHUS SIDETES

The Capture of Demetrius II

The first year of Simon the high priest
of the independent nation of Judea
was the 172nd year
of the Kingdom of the Greeks.   [140 B.C.E.]
This was the year
when Antiochus Sidetes
became king of Syria.

Earlier that year
Demetrius,
king of Syria,
had raised an army to fight Trypho,
the usurper to the crown of Syria,
who had fled to Media.
Demetrius
marched into Media
to capture and kill Trypho.

Arsaces,
king of Persia and Media,
on hearing that Demetrius
had crossed his borders,

became fearful
of Demetrius's full intentions.
So he sent one of his generals
with an army
to take Demetrius alive.
Demetrius was captured and imprisoned.

The Promises of Antiochus Sidetes

Demetrius II's younger brother
was Antiochus, called Sidetes
because he was born
in the city of Side.

Antiochus Sidetes was dwelling
on one of the Islands of the Sea
when he heard the news
that Arsaces had imprisoned his brother,
leaving the Syrian throne vacant.

Antiochus Sidetes
instantly crowned himself
king of Syria
and sent a letter to Simon, saying,

> From King Antiochus
> to Simon, the high priest
> and ruler of the Jewish nation,
> and to the Jewish people:
> Greetings!

MACCABEE

Insofar as certain evil men have usurped
the kingdom of my fathers,
I intend to challenge them
and win it back again,
to restore it to its rightful state.

To that end
I have raised a great army
of mercenaries
and have prepared ships of war.
It is my intent
to go through my kingdom
to avenge myself
on those who destroyed it
and made her cities desolate.

I now confirm upon you
all the honors and gifts
the kings before me granted you:

I give you permission to mint coins
for your own country
with your own stamp.

Regarding Jerusalem and the Temple,
they are yours.

All the weapons that you have made
and all the fortresses that you have built,
keep them.
They are yours.

If there is anything
now owed the king—
and if anything in the future
shall be owed to the king—
the debt is forgiven
from this time forth
and forevermore.

And when the time comes
that we regain our kingdom,
we shall honor you and your nation
and your Temple
and glorify you.
So great will be your glory,
it shall be known
to the ends of the earth!

Trypho Is Surrounded

In the 174th year
of the Kingdom of the Greeks,
Antiochus Sidetes went into Syria,
into the land of his fathers,
with all his armies.
Trypho was greatly outnumbered,
so he fled to the city of Dor-by-the-Sea
in Galilee.

Sidetes camped near Dor
with one hundred twenty thousand foot soldiers

and eight thousand cavalry.
He completely surrounded the town,
by land with troops
and by sea with ships.

He thought to himself,
"How easy to capture Trypho
all by myself!
What need have I of Jews?
Better to sever with them now
and win victory all alone,
than to have to share the spoils
and the glory!"

Antiochus Sidetes camped
outside the city of Dor,
and the next day
he attacked.

Now Simon had sent Sidetes
two thousand select men,
the best warriors of Judea,
carrying many arms
and bearing gifts of silver and gold.

But Sidetes refused the gifts
and sent the Jewish soldiers home.
He then openly broke
all the treaties of the past
between his nation and Judea,
and declared he was no longer
a friend to Israel.

Moreover,
Sidetes sent Athenobius,
one of his friends,
with the following message to Simon:

"You are occupying Jaffa and Gezer,
as well as Jerusalem and its Citadel.
These all belong to me.
And you have destroyed
the territory round about them—
more places that belong to me—
and have inflicted
a great wound on the land.

"Return the cities that you have seized,
along with all the tribute you have taken—
or else give me
five hundred talents of silver.

"Moreover,
for all the harm you have caused,
give me another five hundred talents
or we will attack you."

Athenobius went to Jerusalem
to deliver this message.
When he saw Simon's splendor—
his treasury of silver and gold
and the many people
in attendance upon him—
he was astonished.
Athenobius delivered

the king's message.
Simon listened attentively
and then responded,

"We have not taken
other men's lands.
We have not occupied
other people's territories.
We do not hold
that which belongs to others,
but only the inheritance
of our fathers,
which our enemies
wrongfully possessed
for a limited period of time.
We now once more hold
the inheritance of our ancestors
because the occasion
has arisen to do so.

"As for Jaffa and Gezer,
for which you demand money,
even though these cities did great harm
to our people,
we will give one hundred talents
for them."

Athenobius did not reply,
but turned his back on Simon
and angrily departed,
returning to Antiochus Sidetes.
He reported Jerusalem's splendor
and Simon's response.

392

The king flew into a rage
and began to curse the Jews.
And while he was cursing,
Trypho escaped!

Antiochus Sidetes Begins to Invade Judea

Antiochus Sidetes
made Cendebeus commander
of the sea coast,
assigned him an army
of infantry and cavalry,
and ordered him to march on Judea—
first to capture and strengthen
the city of Kedron,
to fortify its gates
and the walls around it,
and from Kedron to make war
on the Jewish people.

As for himself,
Antiochus set out to catch Trypho.

Cendebeus captured Kedron,
imprisoned the people,
then killed them.
He fortified the city
and stationed cavalry there
and infantry, too,
as the king had ordered him to do.

His plan was to make Kedron
the base for invading Judea,
for many roads
radiating throughout Judea
originated in Kedron.

John, a son of Simon,
was living in the town of Gezer
and learned of Cendebeus's plans.
John left his home
and went up to Jerusalem
to tell his father.

Simon sent
for his son Judah,
named for his brother Judah Maccabee.
Simon said to John and Judah,
"My brothers and I
have from our youth
fought the enemies of our people.
We were victorious,
and we saved Israel.
But I am growing old,
while you, by Heaven's grace,
have grown into fine manhood.
You are the right age to succeed me,
to take my place,
and go forth and fight for our nation,
protecting its freedoms."

Then Simon recruited
twenty thousand warriors with cavalry—

an army to fight Cendebeus.
The army marched to Modin,
the town of Simon's ancestors,
and camped there that night.

When they arose the next morning,
they marched into the plain.
The enemy was waiting.

Judah organized his men.
He placed the cavalry
in the midst of the infantry,
for the enemy's cavalry
greatly outnumbered his own.
Judah shouted the call of alarm,
"Tuh ROO ah,"
and the trumpet sounded,
"RA ta ta, RA ta ta, RA ta ta, TAA."
That terrifying sound
put Cendebeus to flight.

The Death of Trypho

Trypho escaped
to Apamea in Phrygia,
a province with many Jews.
He went there thinking that
Antiochus Sidetes
would not look for him
among the Jews in the Diaspora.

The Jews of Apamea
called the city Kibotus,
which in Greek means "ark,"
because there was a legend
that Noah's Ark had settled
on the distant mountain
overlooking the town.

Trypho learned the story—
how the Creator,
greatly displeased with mankind,
had sent a great flood
to destroy humanity,
but had commanded Noah
to build an ark
to save the animals
and a few good people, too,
to become the parents
of a new breed of good men.

Trypho, wishing to honor Noah
as the savior of mankind,
built a temple facing Mount Kibotus.
He set up in the temple
an image of Noah, a new god
whom he named
Kibotus Soter, "Ark Savior."
And Trypho himself
worshiped the idol in the temple.

His bodyguards
decided it would be safer

to be on the side of Antiochus Sidetes
than on the side of Trypho,
for Trypho seemed unbalanced.
One day they accompanied Trypho to worship.
One of the officers said to him,
"My lord, here you are,
worshiping another Jew."

Trypho explained:
"Noah was not a Jew,
but simply a good man
with no religion
other than a belief in the Creator
and the wish to do
the Creator's will."

The officer said,
"That sounds like a Jew to me!"
Thereupon
the bodyguards drew their swords.

Trypho said to them,
"Hold on, men!
I do not pay you
for service like this!"
Then he drew his own sword—
the same one
with which he slew Jonathan—
and fell upon it,
killing himself.

BALLAD 21
THE DEATH OF SIMON

Ptolemy ben Abubu

There was a certain young Jew
named Ptolemy ben Abubu.
He was a daydreamer,
and he was handsome.

He did not like to work
and did not like to study,
but spent his waking hours
dreaming of growing rich
by doing nothing.

He dreamed, too,
of becoming a Greek,
for he could see
that life was much easier
as a gentile
than as a Jew.
Then the unexpected occurred.

Simon, the high priest,
had a beautiful young daughter
named Maria Anna.

She took one look
at Ptolemy ben Abubu
and instantly fell in love with him.

Simon gave his daughter
in marriage
to Ptolemy ben Abubu.
The wedding and reception
were more lavish
than those given by the gentile kings.

And Simon made Ptolemy
governor of the city of Jericho
and its surrounding fertile plain.
And he also made him
a captain in the army.
And he gave him
plenty of money,
and much silver and gold besides,
for Ptolemy ben Abubu was
after all
the son-in-law of the high priest.

Ptolemy began to dream
of conquering the land of Judea.
He hardly dreamed of anything else.
And soon he was plotting treachery
against Simon, his own father-in-law.

Simon, with his sons
Mattathias and Judah,
decided to make an inspection tour

of the towns and cities of Judea
to be sure they were well governed.
Soon they came to Jericho.

Ptolemy asked Maria Anna,
"Why does your father
come to inspect Jericho?
Doesn't he trust me?"

"Darling," she said,
"certainly he trusts you.
He simply doesn't want
to appear to play favorites."

It was in the 177th year
of the Kingdom of the Greeks   [135 B.C.E.]
in the eleventh month, called Shevat,
that Ptolemy ben Abubu
deceitfully received Simon and his sons
in Jericho.

With his father-in-law's money,
Ptolemy had built a castle in Jericho
for his bride and himself,
and he called the castle "My Dream."
It was here that he received Simon,
the high priest and leader of Israel,
along with his sons and servants.

Ptolemy had prepared a great banquet.
There was plenty to eat,
and on the table
was roasted lamb

and loaves of bread in baskets,
and pitchers of deep red wine.
Servants stood ready
to refill the cups.
Musicians played delightful tunes.

But Ptolemy's men were hiding
and waiting.

After Simon and his sons
had dined too well
and had drunk too much,
Ptolemy ben Abubu
asked the musicians to play
his father-in-law's favorite song.
Simon was touched.
For the first time he believed
Ptolemy actually cared for him.

That song was the signal.
As soon as the song was over,
Ptolemy's men,
with drawn swords,
came forth from their hiding places.
They fell on Simon and his sons
and slew them,
along with their servants.
Then Ptolemy's men
went upstairs to the bedroom
and slew Maria Anna, too.

Thereupon
Ptolemy sent men to Gezer
to kill Simon's son John.
And Ptolemy sent letters
to his friends—
men who called themselves
"defenders of the people"—
to take Jerusalem
and the Temple Mount.
Ptolemy also wrote a letter
to Antiochus Sidetes, king of Syria,
telling him
this was the opportune moment
to invade and conquer Judea.

That is how a son-in-law
paid back his father-in-law's kindness.
And that is how Simon died,
Simon,
the last of the sons of Mattathias.

A New High Priest

Ptolemy's cook
detested Ptolemy
and was fiercely loyal to Simon.
Witnessing the massacre
at the banquet for Simon,
the cook ran ahead to Gezer
to tell Simon's son John
what his brother-in-law Ptolemy

had done,
and to warn him
that Ptolemy was sending men
to slay John, too.

John was stunned,
but when the murderers came,
he was ready.
He killed them.

Afterwards,
John, the son of Simon,
went on to do
many great deeds in Israel.
For war came again to Judea.
The gentiles' determination
to conquer the land
and destroy the children of Israel
did not cease.

John valiantly defended
the country and the people.
His deeds are recorded
in the chronicles of the priesthood,
for he became high priest
after Simon, his father, died.

All five of the sons of Mattathias
now were dead.
All of them had died
in defense of freedom
and religious liberty,

fighting to save their people
and to preserve their way of life
in an independent
and peaceful
nation.

The sons of Mattathias
pursued their work
for thirty years and more.
And after all the campaigns they fought
and all the hardships they endured,
they were victorious.

The struggle of Mattathias
and his sons—
John Gaddi,
Simon Thassi,
Judah Maccabee,
Eleazar Avaran,
and Jonathan Apphus—
infused the children of Israel
with new life
and gave them never-ending hope.

Jews and righteous gentiles
have never forgotten Maccabee
and the other sons of Mattathias
and all the good they did
for Israel
and all humanity.

EPILOGUE

The ballads are over,
but the story goes on.

Just as the old men
sitting at tables
in the town squares
foresaw,
the Romans came.

In wave upon wave,
they conquered Judea,
destroyed the Temple and Jerusalem,
and tortured and killed
many of the children of Israel,
taking survivors back to Rome
as slaves.

But from the ashes of the Temple Mount,
from the rubble of Jerusalem,
from the wilderness of the Judean hills,
from the harbor at Jaffa,
from the shores of Lake Kinneret,
from the beaches of the Mediterranean Sea,
and in the cities of the Diaspora—
Alexandria, Antioch, Athens, Rome,

and everywhere in the civilized world—
some Jews have arisen
to proclaim respect and tolerance
for humanity
in all its diversity.
And some righteous gentiles
have always joined them.

Tyrants continually appear,
trying to make Jews bow down
to their way—the "only" way,
the "true" way—
or to annihilate them.
But to no avail.

The children of Israel kindle lights
for eight days each year
during the holiday of Hanukah
to celebrate the rededication of the Temple,
their survival as a people,
and the rededication of their lives
to justice, liberty, and peace.

There is a light
within the righteous
and courageous spirit
that burns longer than eight days.
It burns forever.

THE END

REFERENCES
FOR QUOTED PASSAGES

As noted in the introduction (particularly pages 1–3 and 13), *Maccabee* is a work of historical fiction based on the four books of Maccabees. In addition to creating dialogue, I have drawn freely from these books without citing source passages except for the quoted letters, proclamations, and statements cited below. *Maccabee* also includes numerous quotations from Hebrew Scriptures and other sources. The references for these quotations are also cited in this section.

My versions of translated passages from Hebrew Scriptures are based upon the Hebrew sources and also upon the standard English translations listed in the Selected Sources. My versions differ from these translations in one major respect: To be faithful to the Hebrew, I have used the symbol *YHV* where the name of God appears in Hebrew Scriptures. This avoids the ambiguity and confusion created by the standard and traditional convention of substituting the word *Lord* for the name of God (see the introduction).

My versions of translated passages from First Maccabees also differ from other translations in one major respect: To be faithful to the author — who, scholars believe, wrote in Hebrew and therefore must have used the word *Torah* — I have in most cases translated the Greek word *nomos* by the Hebrew word *Torah* rather than by the customary English word "law" (see the introduction).

The characters in *Maccabee* occasionally modify a quotation from Hebrew Scriptures — either on purpose or through failure of their memory, because most people in antiquity did not have a copy of Scriptures to consult. I have clearly shown this modification in the relevant references.

Abbreviations Used

Torah: Genesis (Gen), Exodus (Exod), Leviticus (Lev), Numbers (Num), Deuteronomy (Deut).

Books of Prophets: Amos (Amos), Ezekiel (Ezek), Habakkuk (Hab), Isaiah (Isa), Jeremiah (Jer), Micah (Mic), 2 Samuel (2 Sam), Zechariah (Zech), Zephaniah (Zeph).

Sacred Writings: Song of Songs (Song), Psalms (Ps), Ezra (Ezra), Job (Job), Nehemiah (Neh).

Apocrypha: First Maccabees (1 Macc), Third Maccabees (3 Macc).

Ballad 1

p. 52, 1 Macc 1:39-40.

p. 53, Zeph 1:15.

p. 81, Isa 5:25.

p. 82, Ps 130:1.

p. 82, Ps 80:5.

p. 82, "How long, dear God, how long?" is a summary of the many Hebrew complaints to God that begin with "How long . . ." (e.g., Pss 13:1, 79:5, and 94:3; Hab 1:2).

Ballad 2

pp. 95-99, 3 Macc 3:12-29.

pp. 119-121, 3 Macc 7:1-9.

Ballad 3

p. 124, Isa 9:6.

p. 130, Job 1:21.

p. 132, Ps 94:1-3.

p. 135, Ps 139:7-10 (as modified by Mattathias).

pp. 135-36, Ps 115:4-8 (as modified by Mattathias).

p. 138, 1 Macc 2:27.

Ballad 4

    p. 154, Isa 6:3.

    p. 154, Isa 40:6-8.

Ballad 5

    p. 157, Ex 15:11.

    p. 157, Goodman, *The Hanukkah Anthology*, p. 346.

    p. 163, Ps 46:1-3.

Ballad 6

    pp. 169-70, Jer 6:22-23.

    pp. 171-72, "Have mercy . . . are silent" is a prayer that I
        based upon 1 Macc 3:44-45.

    p. 182, Ps 121:1-4.

    p. 182, This is the opening line of many psalms, including
        Pss 106, 118, and 136.

Ballad 7

    p. 185, Isa 44:28-45:6.

    p. 190, Ps 118:26-27.

    p. 190, Gen 1:3.

    p. 190, Deut 6:4.

    p. 191, Deut 6:4.

    p. 191, Ps 100:1-2.

    pp. 191-92, Ps 30.

    pp. 193-94, Ps 118:1-25. (*Hosanna!* means "Save us, we
        pray!")

    p. 194, Exod 20:2.

    p. 195, Isa 56:7.

    p. 195, Ps 67:3-5.

    p. 197, Ps 115:16.

    p. 197, Ps 117.

Ballad 8

p. 199, Ps 59:3-5.

Ballad 9

pp. 209 and 211, *"Ay-lee-yah-hoo hah-nah-vee"* ("Elijah the prophet") is a traditional Hebrew song of unknown origin and age. These English verses ("Our Elijah . . ." and "Heaven took him . . .") are my own free translations.

Ballad 12

p. 239, Ps 79:1-3 (as modified by Alcimus).

Ballad 13

pp. 253-54, 1 Macc 8:23-30.
p. 254, 1 Macc 8:31-32.

Ballad 14

p. 265, 2 Sam 1:19.
p. 265, 2 Sam 1:27.
p. 266, 1 Macc 9:21.

Ballad 15

p. 269, Amos 5:24.
p. 272, Ezra 8:18 and Neh 2:8 (as modified by Jonathan and Simon).
p. 273, Jer 12:1-2 (as modified by Jonathan's soldier).
p. 277, Mic 4:4.

Ballad 16

p. 286, 1 Macc 10:18-20.
p. 287, Lev 23:40.

REFERENCES FOR QUOTED PASSAGES

p. 288, Ps 2:7.
p. 288, 2 Sam 7:14.
p. 289, Ps 23.
p. 289, Num 6:24-26.
pp. 291-94, 1 Macc 10:25-45.
pp. 296-97, 1 Macc 10:52-54.
p. 297, 1 Macc 10:55-56.
p. 300, Mic 6:8.
p. 300, Lev 19:18.

Ballad 18

p. 325, Jer 17:9.
p. 328, Ps 60:11.
p. 333, Gen 29:17.
p. 333, Song 1:15.
p. 341, Mic 4:4.
p. 352, Isa 53:5-7.
p. 352, Isa 42:1-2.

Ballad 19

pp. 358-59, 1 Macc 13:36-40.
p. 360, 1 Macc 13:42.
p. 363, Isa 40:1-2.
p. 364, Isa 52:7.
p. 364, Isa 54:10.
p. 365, Ps 48:1-2.
p. 365, Isa 40:5.
p. 368, Deut 14:1-2.
p. 377, Deut 26:9.
p. 377, Gen 17:7-8.
pp. 378-79, 1 Macc 15:16-20.

SELECTED SOURCES

Primary
(Greek texts and their English translations)

Brenton, Sir Lancelot C. L. *The Septuagint with Apocrypha: Greek and English*. London: Samuel Bagster & Sons, 1851. Reprint, Grand Rapids, MI: Regency Reference Library, 1985 (11th printing). [Contains the four books of Maccabees.]

The First and Second Books of the Maccabees. With commentary by John R. Bartlett. The Cambridge Bible Commentary series. Cambridge: Cambridge University Press, 1973.

Goodspeed, Edgar J. *The Apocrypha: An American Translation*. New York: Random House (Vintage Books), 1959.

Tedesche, Sidney, trans. *The First Book of Maccabees*. With introduction and commentary by Solomon Zeitlin. New York: Harper & Brothers (Dropsie College edition), 1950.

Tedesche, Sidney, trans. *The Second Book of Maccabees*. Edited and with introduction and commentary by Solomon Zeitlin. New York: Harper & Brothers (Dropsie College edition), 1954.

Secondary

Josephus. *Jewish Antiquities*, Books XII–XIV. In *Josephus VII*, translated by Ralph Marcus. Loeb Classical Library. Cambridge, MA: Harvard University Press; London: William Heinemann Ltd., [1933] 1976.

Josephus. *The Life* [an autobiography]. In *Josephus I*, translated by H. St. J. Thackeray. Loeb Classical Library. Cambridge, MA: Harvard University Press; London: William Heinemann Ltd., [1926] 1976.

Moore, George Foot. *Judaism in the First Centuries of the Christian Era: The Age of the Tannaim*. 2 vols. Cambridge, MA: Harvard University Press, [1927] 1955, 1970.

General Reference

Danby, Herbert, trans. and ed. *The Mishnah*. London: Oxford University Press, 1933.

Encyclopaedia Britannica. Thirteenth edition. London and New York: Encyclopaedia Britannica Company, [1910] 1926.

Encyclopaedia Judaica. Jerusalem: Keter Publishing House Ltd., 1971.

Goodman, Philip. *The Hanukkah Anthology*. Philadelphia: The Jewish Publication Society of America, 1976.

The Holy Bible. Revised Standard Version. New York: Thomas Nelson & Sons, 1952.

SELECTED SOURCES

The Holy Scriptures. English text revised and edited by Harold Fisch. Jerusalem: Koren Publishers, 1992.

Isaiah. Hebrew text and English translation with an introduction and commentary by I. W. Slotki. Soncino Books of the Bible. London: The Soncino Press, [1949] 1980.

Liddell, Henry George, and Robert Scott, comps. *A Greek-English Lexicon.* 9th ed., with a revised supplement. Oxford: Clarendon Press/ Oxford University Press, [1843], 1940. Revised supplement, 1996.

The Pentateuch and Haftorahs. 2nd ed. Hebrew text, English translation, and commentary. Edited by J. H. Hertz. London: The Soncino Press, 1960.

The Psalms. Hebrew text and English translation with an introduction and commentary by A. Cohen. Soncino Books of the Bible. London: The Soncino Press, [1945] 1980.

The Torah: A Modern Commentary. Edited by W. Gunther Plaut. New York: Union of American Hebrew Congregations, 1981.

ABOUT THE AUTHOR

HOWARD RUBENSTEIN was born in Chicago in 1931. He received a B.A. degree *magna cum laude* from Carleton College, where he was elected to Phi Beta Kappa and Sigma Xi and won the Noyes Prize for excellence in Greek studies. He received his M.D. degree from the Medical School of Harvard University and has been a physician for over forty years, most of them at Harvard University, but from 1989 to 2000 as a medical consultant to the California Department of Social Services. He has published many articles on medical subjects.

Rubenstein received most of his Jewish education at Anshe Emet Synagogue, Chicago, when Solomon Goldman was rabbi and Moses Silverman was cantor. Other influential mentors there were Ben Aronin and Harry Coopersmith. Rubenstein's formal Jewish education ended with his bar mitzvah in 1944.

In addition to medicine and Judaism in the early centuries before and after the Common Era, Rubenstein's major interests have been modern Judaism and the classics. He and his wife, Judy, have compiled a haggadah, *Becoming Free*, and a Passover songbook, *Songs of the Seder*. Rubenstein's translations from the ancient Greek of Aeschylus' *Agamemnon* and Euripides' *The Trojan Women* have been produced on the stage and published.

Now retired from the practice of medicine, Rubenstein lives with his wife in rural San Diego County, California, where he writes and gardens. The Rubensteins have four grown children.

416